SUMMER RAIN

SUMMER RAIN

Annette Levy-Willard
translated by David Cohen

Psychology News Press
London

First published in 2007
by Psychology News Press
9a Artillery Passage,
London E1 7LN

First published in France in 2007
by Robert Laffont

Set in Palatino
by Keyboards Services, Luton
keyboardserv@aol.com

Printed in England

Distributed by Melia Publishing Services
Godalming
Telephone 01483 869839
melia@melia.co.uk

ISBN
0907633072
978-0907633072

Prologue

'I hate your articles ... I hate you,' the man screams hysterically down my mobile.

'I only write what I see,' I respond calmly. I get as many insulting e-mails as supportive ones which reassures me; I must be doing something right. I reported the war for Libération from the Israeli side of the border but I was also following events inside Lebanon so I had some sense of the suffering there too.

Not that Mr Hysteria cares as he screeches on; 'You never left the bar of your hotel. Or the beach. And anyway it wasn't a war.'

Tell that to the dead and injured, I think.

I hang up – and start writing this book.

Introduction

'Pink sandals?'

Jil has never been on the front line of a war before and she has not come prepared in the shoe department.

'I hadn't reckoned on a war during my holiday,' Jil says.

We'd decided to head off to the front line together – I'm covering events for the Paris paper, *Libération*, Jil for *Radio RCJ*.

We try to buy a map as we fill up with petrol, but the only one we can find is in Hebrew. This is going to be tough. I take the wheel as I have more experience of driving in war conditions.

The statistics show the vagaries of life and death. You have more chance of dying on an Israeli motorway than at the hands of a suicide bomber or a Hezbollah missile. I try to explain to Jil that we can manage without the traditional media fixer – the driver, translator and bodyguard who helps out foreign correspondents.

'Okay, but who is going to translate the news flashes on the radio? We won't know what's going on,' Jil points out.

'Leave the windows down. That way we can hear the sirens.'

Jil is confident in my company because she's been impressed by the anecdotes I've told of wars I have covered. Over the years I have wowed her with tales of my first war in the Lebanon in 1982 when the Israelis pushed on to Beirut and forced Arafat into exile.

And I was there.

It wasn't the same then in 1982, I say to myself, but it was a pretty similar cock-up.

The road north to Lebanon flows easy. Driving is a real pleasure.

3

The stunning Mediterranean coast is empty. Magnificent surf crashes on beautiful beaches but there is not one parasol and not one tourist in sight. The cafés and petrol stations are closed, the trains are not running and there are no busses, either.

In fact, the only signs of life are feline. Cats are the only creatures still out. Great species us humans, we flee the incoming Katyusha rockets, abandon our pets and let them face the missiles.

Speaking to her listeners in Paris, Jil explains we are driving on what seems to be a motorway for VIPs. She's very calm.

When we get to the end of the motorway, we see the capital of northern Israel, Haifa. The town sparkles round the bay. Luxury apartments cover half of Mount Carmel. The stunning golden dome of the Bahia Temple gleams in the sunshine, a symbol of the tolerance that is part of the city's history. Jews and Arabs have lived in Haifa in something that resembles peace and, even, a measure of harmony for generations. But it's a ghost town now. No one is on the streets, no one is driving, and the harbour is dead quiet too.

We hunch over our Hebrew map as Jil gives me directions. We're trying to find the Headquarters of the Israeli Army in the Nof Hotel on Mount Carmel. A mob of TV trucks with their antennae pointing to the sky tells us we have reached Media Central. On the hotel terrace, overlooking the bay, the world's war correspondents, TV's finest, are gathered. They've donned their impressive body armour and khaki shirts. Heroes and heroines of the airwaves are launching into their excited introductions. 'Yes, dear viewers we're braving the bullets for you.' Then;

'*And we are live from Haifa,*' they trumpet.

I head past the crowd into a basement where a press conference is taking place. I make for the front row. An Israeli general with a Japanese sounding name, Ido Neuhustan, is giving the briefing. He explains with stupendous complacency that everything is going to plan, the army is marching forward, but – forward to where, exactly?

4

Introduction

'There's no question of going beyond a few kilometers into South Lebanon,' insists Le General, who is Commander in Chief of the Northern Region. 'There's also no question of calling up the reservists or sending in the infantry.'

No question? Can this be good strategy, to broadcast to the world how far you will – and won't – go?

Of course the mighty Israeli military must know what it is doing. But the hacks are pressing.

'Why bomb Beirut?' asks one journalist. His accent suggests he is from the Middle East. 'What could be the purpose of hitting civilians?'

'We're targeting the terrorists of Hezbollah who unfortunately are hiding in the middle of the civilian population,' the general replies laconically. He seems suddenly exhausted by the mere act of speaking.

Everything he and other military spokesmen say is utterly predictable. I could have written it myself. It makes me wonder if it was worth the hassle of coming here. I decide not to take in the rest of the briefing and take my leave of the forest of microphones pointed at the all-too-wooden military spokesmen. I go and join Jil sunbathing on the terrace.

The sky is clear, the panoramic view magnificent. Below us lie the quiet city, the blue sea and the still port.

'Nothing to do except get a tan,' Jil smiles. She's relaxed, as ever, on the phone to Paris.

Then the sirens blare – a strident sound, shattering our mood.

We know the rules of this game. The sirens blare a minute before Hezbollah rockets fired from Lebanon crash somewhere near us, possibly very near us, perhaps into our cocktails.

We have 60 seconds to move. The choice is; stay on the terrace where we may see the spot the missile hits, hoping it won't be too close to us, or scamper down to the underground shelter in the hotel.

Reasonable people scamper. The real men or real fools – the military, the journalists, Jil and I, assume the 'we don't care

5

and we don't scare' attitude. Danger, what danger? We don't move an inch. We relax for sixty seconds and then, on the button, the missile screeches through the sky, trailing a plume of white. Seconds later, the rocket smashes into the bottom of the hill a few hundred metres down from us. The noise is brutal.

Fifteen seconds ago we were calm, cool, sipping our cocktails. Now we feel less cool and our situation seems less funny.

We leap into the car and hurtle towards the Hadar area near the port where the rocket struck. Jil jokes at my Formula 1 style driving, but the Schumachers of this world know where they're going and have practiced all the straights and corners. I've never driven through these narrow Haifa streets before.

All joking stops when we see how much the missile has destroyed. Windows and walls have been smashed. Fragments of glass litter the street, all thanks to the Raad missile – it means thunder in Arabic. The Raad is an Iranian weapon, which can hit a target 100 kilometres away.

The Raad has left a trail of destruction. Everywhere on the street, on the pavement, in the entrances to buildings, there are nasty ball bearings. The missile was packed with them and pieces of iron. Haifa is terrorized. Thousands of people who live here have fled.

'Ugly these little nuggets,' says Jil.

She's upset as she picks up a handful of ball bearings.

Introduction

A Note on Distances

The distance from Haifa to Beirut is about 70 miles, the same as from London to just north of Birmingham.

In the days of the British mandate, a train used to run from Cairo to Beirut via Tel Aviv.

If you boarded the train at 6 p.m. in Haifa, you could be in Beirut for dinner at 9 p.m.

It takes Israel's jets 8 minutes to fly from the Israeli border to Beirut.

There is only 60 seconds warning of incoming missiles because they have to travel the distance from Brighton to London or less.

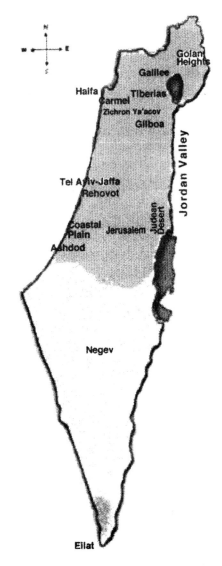

The 'Biblical' land of Israel including Gaza and the West Bank

July 9

Our holiday in Israel had started calmly – if you can describe a film festival as calm.

We were at the Jerusalem International Film Festival; the cinemathèque is opposite the walls of the Old City. The festival provides a unique forum for Israeli and Palestinian filmmakers to meet, screen movies and argue film. It is an excellent place to take the temperature of the Middle East.

The festival is very left wing, iconoclastic and full of wry humour. A few years ago it hosted a day of short films. For one, an intrepid director took his camera on to the streets of Tel Aviv and asked the supreme candid camera question:

'Are you ready to sleep with Arafat if that would bring peace to the Middle East?'

Most Israelis were willing to make this supreme sacrifice with the redoubtable Chairman and said 'yes' – though with little enthusiasm.

One young man went so far as to say: 'I am ready for sodomy with the man if that gets us lasting peace.'

We festival folk, like film festival crowds all over the world, are very self-sufficient but a bit chaotic. We run from show to show to make sure we miss nothing, not one frame in the vital battle for who will win best film, best actress, let alone best make up. Our eyes glued to the screens, we don't notice the small event, the tiny ripple in the pool, the blood on the stair, which triggers everything that follows.

I'm at the Festival with my family, including my teenage son, Tom, who has turned up at the Hotel Mount Zion with full surfing regalia, magic surfboard and all. The Holy

The Lebanese villages at the heart of the action

City of Jerusalem is actually 70 kilometres from the sea and the very distinguished-looking Palestinian Maitre D's are not fazed. They cope, day in day out, with American orthodox Jews who come to the Wailing Wall to wail about the state of the world. So what trouble can one teenager with a surfboard be?

As we watch film after film, life potters amiably on; tourists have not cancelled their holidays; young men who have just finished their army service are planning trips to India. They don't imagine for one second that they will have to pick up their machine guns before too long.

In 2005, the previous summer, I had reported for *Libération* how the army evicted the settlers from the Gaza strip. Not one Israeli left in Gaza, I remembered thinking that had to be good news. If Palestinians and Israelis could ignore each other for a little while and each concentrate on their side of the border, maybe there would be some progress towards peace.

I had brought my son to Gaza on my journo's journey back in 2005 and waxed lyrical.

'Look at the wonderful beaches,' I said to Tom. 'Maybe one day this will be like Cannes: tourists, a casino, high rise hotels.'

My son was fascinated by the behaviour of the Israeli army as they removed the settlers, many of whom left in tears. He was less interested in my visions of Utopia.

History did no favours for those of us who hoped for Utopia. In 2006, Hamas won the election for the Palestinian Parliament and Hamas does not recognize the state of Israel.

Crude rockets, made in Gaza, continued to slam across the border after the army withdrew. Hundreds hit the small Israeli town of Sderot just to guarantee there could not be ... hell, no one was talking permanent peace, but not even a truce.

Then on the night of June 25, 2006, a Palestinian commando unit dug a tunnel out of Gaza and slipped over the border into Israel. The unit emerged at an army sentry post in Kerem

Shalom. Alert the sentries were not. The Israeli soldiers were asleep in their open tank. The lookouts had failed to look out – and they paid for it with their lives. The soldiers didn't even have time to get out their weapons. Two were killed; one was wounded and a fourth man was kidnapped. The hostage was a 19-year-old Corporal, Gilad Shalit, who was doing his military service.

Gilad Shalit – the teenager who started a war. The ransom demanded was the release of hundreds of Palestinian prisoners from Israeli jails. Some of them had been found guilty of acts of terrorism, including murder.

The kidnapping of Gilad Shalit was a warning of the failures to come in the 33-day war. But neither I, at the Film Festival, nor anyone else, it must be said, realised that on this significant day.

The 33-day war would dent the invincible image of the Israeli military revealing a catalogue of failures. Perhaps the greatest surprise was the staggering ineptitude of the so-called intelligence agencies. Their surveillance of Palestinian militants had clearly been a joke. Israel's legendary intelligence agency, Mossad, had not even noticed that men were digging a tunnel from Gaza. And digging a tunnel that runs for 600 metres is complicated and time-consuming, requiring significant manpower and organization. After the Yom Kippur war of 1973, Israel was supposed to be always vigilant.

The tunnel to the sentry post at Kerem Shalom was not the only one. The border between Gaza and Egypt has as many holes as a good Gruyère.

A similar failure of intelligence was to become all-too apparent on the South Lebanon border. There, Israel's super spies had failed to notice that Hezbollah, the Party of God, had built bunkers, secret passageways and labyrinths. Somehow Israel's formidable intelligence agencies had not recruited any agents smart enough to find out that Hezbollah had also acquired Russians missiles called Fagot and Kornet. These could even destroy the indestructible Israeli tank – the famous Merkava 4.

Or if the spies knew it, they forgot to tell the Army High Command.

Hezbollah was not, incidentally, keeping its plans secret. To assist the comatose Israeli intelligence agencies, one of its leaders even issued a direct warning. Haj Hazzan, one of the 12 Hezbollah members of the 128-strong Lebanese Parliament, said on the record that Haifa could soon 'be one of the targets we aim for'.

Moments after Gilad Shalit was kidnapped, intelligence officers briefed the press with bravado.

'We know *exactly* where the kidnapped soldier is,' they boasted. Oh really?

Then, more incompetence from an army that was supposed to be supremely competent.

The 'greatest army in the world' did not move fast enough to stop the commando unit that snatched Gilad Shalit. The Corporal's kidnappers walked back to Gaza – a 2 hour hike – without being stopped by the military.

Israeli politicians reacted with all the grace of a rhino stung by a wasp.

The rhino does not negotiate. The wasp is a menace to civilization. The wasp must be exterminated.

'No, we do not negotiate with terrorists. We refuse on principle any exchange of prisoners. No means no,' insisted the government of Ehud Olmert. He became Prime Minister only because Ariel Sharon slipped into a coma in January 2005 and then won an election, albeit against a weak opposition.

Olmert chose to revenge himself on Gaza. The Operation, curiously, was dubbed 'Summer Rain'. One has to wonder why the colonels and generals like to give their attacks such romantic titles. Do they think a military operation should sound like a perfume? We shall destroy the enemy in operation Chanel No 5. In retaliation, Israeli planes *summer-rained*, or bombed, the bridge and main road leading to Gaza's electricity station.

'Why?' We ask at a press conference.

'To force them to release Gilad Shalit,' replies the government spokesman, mysteriously.

Cutting off electricity so the fridges don't work in the middle of the summer? A uniquely original strategy. Just how is that going to help free Shalit?

The attack on the refrigerators of Gaza, the demolition of buildings and the assassination attempts against members of Hamas show that the rhino can stamp his feet and blow his horn. But all the sound and fury has the impact we sceptics in the press corps expect.

None at all.

Hamas, of course, knows the sentimental nature of Israeli society and manipulates it. Israel has to bring back all its soldiers – dead or alive. In 2004, the government 'paid' not just to recover one living hostage but also the bodies of three Israelis kidnapped in Lebanon.

The price was steep in 2004 – 400 Palestinians and 23 Lebanese. The Germans acted as intermediaries.

Today it is clear that Israel will have to pay an even higher price for the return of one living Gilad Shalit – at least 1,000 Palestinian prisoners.

Shalit had been taken to Gaza which is a long way from Jerusalem – not so much geographically, but spiritually, emotionally and intellectually distant. At the film festival, we follow a different war. By July 9, tension is mounting. The warring parties are the French and the Italians. We have abandoned cinema to watch the World Cup final. We are divided into those who are for Zidane and those who are for the Italians. Both sides have consumed large quantities of beer and red wine by the time Zidane signs off with his head butt. That, and losing the final, depresses the French who go back to their hotels to sleep off the catastrophe, while the Italians continue to drink and celebrate.

July 9

The morning after we resume our lovely festival life: a dip in the pool followed by important debates on aspects of cinema. We do our best to avoid the many films about Jews, concentration camps and deportations.

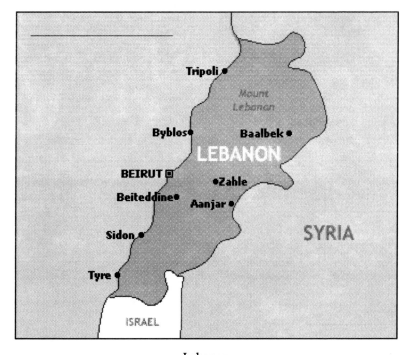

Lebanon

July 12

Before going to see our first film of the day, we cast an eye on the news, but we don't think it is going to affect our plans to sample more cine culture.

This Wednesday morning, armed militants come down from the green hills of South Lebanon in a show of strength by Hezbollah, the modestly-named 'Party of God'. Until now Hassan Nasrallah, leader of Hezbollah, hasn't exactly been a household name. The only people who know about him, in fact, are university specialists in Middle Eastern politics, his enemies (mostly American and Israeli), and his Syrian and Iranian paymasters. The world's intelligence agencies no doubt have extensive files on him, but he is pretty much unknown on the worldwide stage and web.

But now Hassan ascends to the podium and takes up the laurels and cudgels of No 1 Super Revolutionary – a position left vacant by the death of Arafat, the ageing of Fidel Castro and the disappearance of Bin Laden into some grotto near the Khyber Pass.

Nasrallah has a marketing script that Satan could have written.

At dawn rockets start to pour down on the kibbutzim and towns of Northern Israel. People flee into their shelters.

Many readers of this book will know the history of the conflict but some will not. In 1982 there was an attempt to kill Shlomo Argov, the Israeli ambassador in London. The ambassador was badly wounded at the Dorchester Hotel. In retaliation the then-Israeli Prime Minister, Menachem Begin and his Defence Minister, Ariel Sharon, sent the Israeli army into Lebanon and took Beirut. The victory turned to ashes as Sharon stood by and encouraged

Lebanese Christians to massacre 3,000 unarmed women and children in the refugee camps of Sabra and Chatilla. This remains one of the great shames of Israeli history. Finally, in 2000, the Israelis pulled out of southern Lebanon, though they held on to a buffer zone of some 40 square kilometres known as Sheeba Farms.

After the Israelis left, the Syrians controlled Lebanon. It seems that whatever happens, the Lebanese must not be allowed to govern their own country.

In 2004, United Nations Resolution 1559 tried to re-establish the authority of the Lebanese government over its own land and international pressure forced the Syrian army to leave the country. The UN Resolution also asked for all arms shipments to terrorist groups to be stopped.

Far from accepting the United Nations Resolution, however, Hezbollah built up an impressive arsenal in southern Lebanon. They acquired rockets far more powerful than the Qassams that can only fly a few kilometres from Gaza to Sderot.

On the morning of July 12, Hezbollah's missiles are a diversion. While everyone worries about them, a group of Hezbollah fighters open a hole in the barbed wire border-fence and enter Israel. Hezbollah are well informed, it seems. They are ready to attack an Israeli motorized patrol in the area.

Hezbollah succeed in killing three soldiers and taking two others hostage; then, they take their precious hostages across the border back into Lebanon.

Two hours later an Israeli tank crosses the border to rescue the kidnapped soldiers, but it is hit by another missile. Israeli soldiers try to help their comrades trapped in the tank and discover they are already dead. The rescue party itself is pinned down by Hezbollah fire.

Eight Israelis die – and it's not yet 10 a.m. Heavy losses for a morning that dawned quite ordinary.

The taking of two hostages by Hezbollah means they have bested their great rival, Hamas. Hamas only managed to kidnap

Gilad Shalit. Now Hezbollah have got Ehud Goldwasser and Elded Regen, civilians who were doing their annual tour of military service.

Hezbollah, the modern Shiite militia, announces its triumph live on its TV chain, Al Manar: *'According to its duties, Hezbollah has decided to liberate prisoners and detainees. The party has succeeded in capturing two soldiers on the border with occupied Palestine.'*

Occupied Palestine, for which read the *State of Israel*, created in 1947 by United Nations resolution 181.

The Hezbollah commando unit, which has gone back into Lebanon with its human booty, is probably holed up in a bunker or safe in Syria.

We don't know it at the time, but another war is being fought, between Israelis. As the tanks roll into Lebanon, the Israeli army asks the intelligence services to hand over all the secret files they have accumulated on Hezbollah's bunkers, tunnels and fortifications. The top secret Intelligence Committee on Source Information replies that the army can't be allowed to get the secret information because *it is too secret*. So Israeli troops go into battle without the latest information on the enemy.

And I'm fighting my own war on the internet.

When I gave up my holiday to report on the war, I was astonished by the many abusive e-mails that came in. Most were from people who clearly hadn't read my articles at all, or skimmed them free on the web, so they could snipe back without making the effort to stick a letter in an envelope or lick a stamp. One particularly aggressive e-mail stood out.

'You write that Hezbollah took 2 Israeli soldiers. So what? Bully for Hezbollah. The soldiers shouldn't have been in Lebanon! What were they doing there?'

They were in their own country, on their side of the border, on the Blue Line, as recognized by the international community, I blast back, and never hear from him again.

But this exchange is a sign of the media war to come. A

while later, I read an article by Karim Emiler Bitar, editor in chief of a review named after ENA, the prestigious School of Administration, *ENA hors le murs* – so this is not a light or superficial publication. Bitar offers a long and apparently historically sophisticated analysis. As I read I have to rub my eyes in wonder. He states:

'In response to this operation by Hezbollah, Israel destroys the airport in Beirut, imposes a naval blockade and bombs the country causing more than 80 civilian deaths. It is only after this that Hezbollah starts to strike at innocent civilians in the north of Israel.'

The facts of July 12 are clear:

Hezbollah starts early. At dawn their rockets pour down on the kibbutzim and towns of northern Israel where the 'innocent civilians' sleep. And it dispatches a commando unit to attack a patrol inside Israel, not inside Lebanon.

That is how it started. The history of these 33 days of war is cruel enough. We don't need to airbrush the image of Hezbollah, as ever so moral and, indeed, pacifist terrorists who just had to blast rockets at innocent civilians, after wicked Israel started bombing Lebanon.

Hezbollah's provocations came first. But the vital question is – how intelligent was the Israeli response?

Not very, I shall argue.

But as it has two hostages, Hezbollah is in the driving seat. The package on the table – great to speak of human beings as 'packages' – now contains three kidnapped Israelis.

The price of said package has gone sky high. Hezbollah want several thousand Palestinian prisoners in return as well as three Lebanese. The most famous prisoner they demand is Samir Al Qanter, who has been in jail for 27 years. When he was sixteen, Samir was part of a commando unit that slipped into the coastal town of Nahariya, three kilometers from the Lebanese border. The commandos burst into the home of an ordinary Israeli family, snatching the father and his four-year-old daughter. They dragged them to the beach where they shot the man and killed his little girl by shattering her skull against the rocks. Her mother had hidden with her other child, a two-year-old girl, who died of asphyxiation in a cupboard.

But the local news and the activities of Hezbollah do not interrupt our fun at the film festival. And I am one of the happy few to get an invitation to the designed-to-the-eyeballs residence of the French Ambassador for Bastille Day, July 14.

Only the party is held on July 12.

This year Bastille Day falls on a Friday, the Sabbath, and no embassy in Israel can dream of putting on a serious celebration on Shabbat, because as soon as the sun sets, the esteemed rabbis can't be partying or even eating kosher canapés. They have to be praying in synagogue. So the Ambassador has changed the date of Bastille Day and we are to party on the 12th.

The Ambassador's residence is in the old Arab town of Jaffa, which Napoleon burnt down during his 1798 campaign. Napoleon's aim was his usual one – to make sure everyone knew he was the biggest beast in Europe and to kick the British King, Queen, Empire and Horatio Nelson, in the crotch.

At the Ambassador's residence all the journalists are waiting for the guest of honour, Prime Minister Ehud Olmert. He does not come. He has to forego the brie and excellent Bordeaux to stay in his office in Jerusalem and listen to his generals. Dan Halutz, the Chief of Staff, explains they do have a plan to finish Hezbollah once and for all. It seems the romantics who gave us 'Operation Summer Rain' were off work when this one was drawn up. Less subtly, it is code-named 'Exterminator'. Frustrated generals had to keep this master plan in a drawer for years; they began to despair of ever being given the chance to use it. But helpful Hezbollah is now making it possible for them to take Exterminator out of mothballs.

'It's *war*,' says the French Ambassador, Gerard Araud, as he shakes my hand.

Araud seems more aware of the here and now than the military attachés and other dignitaries – not to mention their women, who are dressed in blue and pink outfits. I could almost believe we were back in colonial Africa, fly-whisking mosquitoes. On the television screen the French Foreign Minister, Philippe Douste Blazy, is talking – the name is a little odd in French, and it is virtually impossible to resist the temptation to nickname him 'Minister Blazing Dust'. The guests seem reassured.

On his balcony in Jaffa, the ambassador seems more and more preoccupied. The skyscrapers of Tel Aviv, the Semitic 'city that never sleeps', light up. A hundred years ago it did not exist.

I have a last glass of wine after our national anthem and leave for Jerusalem to catch the evening show at the Festival.

Jerusalem is not usually a vibrant city by night, but now no one is sleeping. The atmosphere on the terrace which looks out on to the magical walls of the Old City has changed. I don't hear any of the puff profound conversations about the significance of the close-up in Japanese cinema or the usual existential angst piddle of cine-fests. (Or what people really care about – who will they meet? What time is the dinner with Polanski? Am I invited?)

The audience that comes out of the last show has more substantial worries; they want to know what's going on.

What is going on is that the Israeli Air Force is bombing the runways at Beirut Airport as well as roads and bridges in Lebanon. The air force is also attacking the supposed Hezbollah bunkers. Something major is happening.

July 13

The night of the 12th to the 13th is long.

One of my friends at the Festival is furious. His car has been broken into yet again and the radio stolen. The windows are shattered. I noticed broken glass every morning in the Cinematheque Parking and, being careful, parked my rental car close to the hotel entrance where the security guards could keep an eye on it.

The news reaches us in cinema-land where we're eating, drinking and talking. War or not war? That is the question. People hang about hoping it will be like a movie. When the lights come back up, everything will return to dull normality. But when Israel wakes up, the situation is neither dull nor normal.

For most of its history Israel has elected military heroes as politicians. Moshe Dayan, Ariel Sharon, Ehud Barak, Yitzhak Rabin. Even Binyamin 'Bibi' Netanyahu held the rank of Colonel. Now the country is governed by a coalition whose members have not won many campaign medals.

'The Cabinet is full of ex-lawyers, ex-journalists, and former trade unionists. These civilians have to decide how to wage this war,' says my friend Alex who is very left-wing and a sharp, lucid analyst of the situation. 'They will want to show they have balls.'

Indeed.

In Israel, where the military is the one of the only institutions held in high public esteem, leaders without command experience have a lot to prove. And fast. It does not take more than an hour for these 'civilians' to grab their arrows, put on their war paint and whirl their axes around their heads.

I know that there was a cabinet meeting on the evening of the 12th. But no one has managed to find out who said what. The Israeli press is very sharp and tenacious but not one journalist has managed to get anyone who was present at that meeting to leak what happened.

It is only three months later, when Olmert addresses the country on Rosh Hashanah, the Jewish New Year, that he will reveal what was discussed at that cabinet meeting on the first day of the war. 'Every member of the government voted for the operation,' he claims.

'And Shimon Peres?' The question comes from a well informed journalist. Peres, who shared the Nobel Peace Prize with Arafat and Rabin for the Oslo accords, is widely respected in the West and seen as Israel's voice of reason. But he is a complex figure: a protégé of David Ben-Gurion, he served for many years at the heart of the defence establishment and played a key part in making Israel a nuclear power. At times a peacemaker, he has never been a pacifist.

'Shimon only asked one question,' we learn, and that was: 'What will happen *after the air strikes?*'

Good question. No answer. The government and the military chiefs think bombings from the air will do the trick.

Alex and I drink an excellent bottle of red wine from the Golan Heights, which were taken from the Syrians in the 1967 war.

'You must understand the psychological shock, the anxiety,' says Alex. After a few glasses of red, he is gloomy. 'It is a crisis of confidence. Now that the all-powerful Israeli army has been surprised on its own territory by two small guerilla raids by ragtag militias. Tsahal is no longer *invulnerable.*' Tsahal is the affectionate name used by Israelis to refer to the army.

The morning papers reflect public opinion and put the same question Alex did. It's clear he thinks the situation is serious, but not so serious that he will miss his weekly trip to the Dead Sea to take a refreshing mud bath.

July 13

*Our famous army … best in the world … technologically tops …
the shield that has allowed the Hebrew state to survive,* the Op Ed
pieces say of Tsahal. But Hezbollah's audacity stirs the anxiety,
never deeply buried in Israel's collective unconscious, that was
expressed so well by David Ben Gurion:
  *'Even if Israel wins 50 wars we will not defeat the Arab world
but the Arabs have to win only one war to destroy Israel.'*
  The mighty Israeli army has allowed itself to lose one soldier to
a rag-tag commando unit from Gaza. Even worse, Hezbollah have
had the chutzpah to cross the border, attack us, kill eight soldiers
and take two hostages. How is it possible? How is it possible?
  The kidnappings could have been prevented, it will emerge
eventually. But the intelligence services didn't even have the
intelligence to read what Hezbollah had been saying. The
organisation had announced that one of their plans was to
kidnap Israeli soldiers.
  But the day after the first attack, no one is ready to examine
the military blunders. The country has just one idea in mind
– to thump the enemy, to pulverize it with a show of force so
terrible that it will make it very clear you do not mess with
Goliath Israel. You may, dear neighbours, dream your dark
dreams of destroying the Jewish State…
  Dream on, dream on!
  The government of the non-military with balls chooses the
macho line: 'We do not negotiate with terrorists and we demand
the immediate return of our soldiers who were taken hostage.'
Hamas and Hezbollah just need to learn one lesson – you do
not trifle with the lives of Israeli soldiers.
  Everyone agrees on this hard line. Or nearly everyone.
  I go to see Danny Yatom, the former head of Mossad, Israel's
famous secret service. He is sceptical and says he would take
a more conciliatory tone.
  'An exchange of prisoners is sometimes the only solution
when all the military options are impossible,' he says calmly.
And he knows what he is talking about.

Impossible?

Yatom's view is very much a minority one today. For now, the military solution seems excellent – especially to the military, who have convinced the government of the merits of their fabulous plan.

The Army Chief of Staff is Dan Halutz, who previously headed the Air Force. Halutz's philosophy is simple. You fight the war from high altitude on sophisticated screens like a video game. He sends planes to bomb Beirut airport and Hezbollah's Al Manar television station. (Al Manar will continue on air throughout the war, since they had the genius to make contingency plans so they could broadcast from different places.) Halutz also sends planes to blast the southern suburbs of Beirut where Hezbollah has its Headquarters. Revenge will be swift and efficient. The Chief of Staff brims with confidence.

So the end of the first day finds Halutz in his Tel Aviv headquarters. At midnight he dispatches his F15s to destroy the enemy and break its will. Then he waits. Thirty minutes later, he gets the report he hoped for from the Squadron Leader in charge of the attack.

'We have destroyed 54 rocket launchers,' the Squadron Leader tells him, adding, 'these were the launchers that could fire the long distance Zelzal rockets that threaten Tel Aviv.'

Mission Accomplished. No more rockets will rain on plucky Israel. But 'mission accomplished' is a dangerous phrase in war today. Halutz should have remembered the scene in 2003. George Bush, wearing an Air Force jacket, lands on an American aircraft carrier in the Gulf. Like Winston Churchill, Bush flashes the V for Victory sign and smiles at the waiting cameras. 'Mission accomplished,' Bush declares to his people, thinking the Iraq war is over when, in fact, it is just beginning.

Bush and Halutz would have done better to remember the eloquent caution of Churchill after El Alamein. 'It is not the end, it is not the beginning of the end. It is, however, the end of the beginning.'

Halutz seems to suffer an attack of the Bush-es and does not hesitate for one second. The Chief of Staff picks up the hot line phone and rings the Prime Minister at his home in Jerusalem.

Prime Minister Olmert is waiting for the call – and waiting in style. He is smoking a cigar, perhaps because he thinks the Churchillian touch will play well.

'WE HAVE WON THE WAR,' says the Chief of Staff.

But just to be sure of the victory, the military also drop a small group of elite paratroopers into southern Lebanon. These commandos will clean out the nest of terrorists in the hills and villages overlooking the border.

But the plan goes wrong. Hezbollah are waiting for the commandos in bunkers in the village of Maroun-al-Ras, one kilometer inside Lebanon. The Israelis take fire from all sides.

The General Staff, which has just won the war in half an hour, panic. They now dispatch yet another elite commando unit, the famous Egoz Unit, to rescue the surrounded paras. But Hezbollah has done its homework and is expecting that kind of response. The Egoz Unit itself is ambushed – making for yet another disaster. Hezbollah apparently don't know the rules of Arab-Jewish wars.

The Israeli army has had a shock. It has discovered that the enemy is well-equipped, well-trained and well-motivated. This is not a band of suicidal terrorists in scruffy jeans who squabble amongst themselves.

'They wear smart uniforms, are very determined and stay calm under fire,' Jonathan tells me. He managed to escape from Maroun-al-Ras. He is 22 years old and in a state of shock, which is no surprise, as he has carried dead comrades in body bags back to 'safety' on his shoulders.

'We marched at night – we always carry out operations at night and we are equipped with night vision equipment so we can shoot in the dark,' Jonathan tells me. 'At four in the morning Hezbollah ambushed us in an orchard, attacked us and threw grenades. It ended up in hand-to-hand combat, we really could see the whites of their eyes. They are no cowards – and we're not either.'

The Israeli units expected to be fighting for a few hours and, already, they have been fighting longer.

Today Israeli bombs killed 47 Lebanese civilians, mainly in areas occupied by the militias of the Party of God.

Hezbollah has shown that it can strike at the heart of Israel. Its missiles can reach Nahariya, where a woman is killed in her room, and Safed. Safed, up in the hills, is the old centre of Jewish mysticism. Jews lived here before, during, and after the time of Christ. It has also become something of an artist's colony, and has not been hit by a rocket since 1973. The mayhem the rockets cause remind us that Party of God militia are not interested in the Biblical prophecy: 'And Judah and Israel dwelt safely, every man under his vine and under his fig tree, from Dan even to Beersheba, all the days of Solomon.'

The Bible, of course, did not give women vine and fig tree rights.

The first 24 hours of this Operation – no one in the government or the military is using the word 'war' – have been surprising.

For Lebanon the Operation is a very bad surprise. The country is being punished for having looked the other way while the Party of God seized control of much of the South – and the Party of God is, of course, remote-controlled by Iran.

For Israel it is an unhappy surprise to discover that an all too real army is squatting on its border, a legion of guerillas who can peer into the windows of the House of Israel. This new-fangled army sits, invisible in its bunkers with thousands of high-tech missiles: the Farj with a range of 70 kilometres, the Zelzal which can fly 120 kilometres. Both have been provided by Iran to attack the 'Zionist enemy'.

In time it will become clear that Nasrallah did not expect Israel's response to be so drastic. He did not expect, we shall discover, to unleash the dogs of war by the small cross border raid. Thirty two days later, right after the ceasefire, Nasrallah records an interview for Al-Manar Television.

'We did not think that the capture of two soldiers would lead *immediately* to war – and to a war of such an extent,' he says to a television crew from his hidden lair somewhere. (He knows the Israelis are still dreaming of killing him.)

By the end of the war, Nasrallah has become an international star and is willing to be self-critical. He also assumes the role of the compassionate leader who is ever so sorry to have been the cause of so much death.

'You ask me: *"If I had known on the 12th of July that the operation would lead to such a war, would I have started it?"* He goes on, trying to look sincere, making good eye contact with the television lens.

'I say no, absolutely NO. Absolutely no!'

Unfortunately, I was not invited to this interview. Did he give it in his bunker or in Damascus or in some cave or in Teheran? Or simply at a friend's house in Beirut?

Wherever, I'd have liked to put the obvious question to him.

'If you regret the loss of life, why, as Secretary General of Hezbollah, did you order your militias to attack Israelis on Israeli territory on July 12? What was the goal of the operation?'

Since I was not present at this interview, I have to reply for the Secretary General and rely on his routine line – resistance:

'We have to liberate Lebanon from the Israeli Occupation,' he usually says.

As occupations go, the Israeli occupation of Lebanon is rather limited. The only area of Lebanon under Israeli control is the Sheeba Farms 'buffer zone' and even Sharon swore never to re-enter the Lebanon. But the charter of the Party of God is resolute: 'We remain firm in our strategy for eliminating the state of Israel from the map.'

But maybe Nasrullah was telling the truth. Maybe he did not want a war now. Fifteen days before the war started, at a conference, he predicted quiet summer holidays, bikinis in

Beirut. No one wanted to discourage the tourists flocking back to Lebanon.

So why did Nasrullah change his mind? Was it because his Iranian paymasters were irritated by United Nations resolutions which aimed to stop them building an atomic bomb? Is it a complete coincidence that the Security Council gave Iran an ultimatum to stop enriching uranium by July 12?

War between Israel and the Arabs would push Iran's nuclear ambitions down the news agenda and on to the back pages. So Hezbollah waves a red rag at the Israeli bull, not thinking that the bull might lower its horns and charge.

And what do we know about bulls? They have more testosterone than brains.

July 14

In France le tout Paris is watching the last garden party that Jacques Chirac will give at the Elysee on Bastille Day.

Here, no one could care less. Israeli planes bomb Lebanon, but the elite units don't manage to dislodge Hezbollah or its rocket launchers. The missiles still thud across the border.

'I am supposed to be on holiday but I must go see what is happening on the border,' I say, refusing the tempting option of the pool followed by screenings.

'Alone?' I'm asked.

'Why not alone? I know the way, I did it in 1982 – and hey, there are signposts. You head north.'

'There weren't any missiles then and Hezbollah did not exist. The situation is not the same. A small girl and her grand mother were killed this morning by a rocket which hit their house. I'll drive.'

It's good advice. I accept the offer made by the father of my children.

Now starts the comedy of Mum and Dad go to war but we must not tell the children.

'We're going to Tel Aviv,' we tell the kids. We have decided to lie to avoid stress and melodramatic scenes. I can imagine how my teenage son Tom would react. 'No, don't do that to us. Don't you love us? You'll die and we'll be sent to the orphans' homes.' Or: 'We'll be in therapy for the rest of our lives.'

Actually, they're a little too old to be sent to an orphanage.

So having not told our children the truth, we get in the car and head in the direction opposite to Tel Aviv. We take the

Summer Rain

A detailed map of Israel, part of the West Bank and the Golan Heights

splendid road towards the Dead Sea which was built for the settlers of Maale Adumim – a huge colony which the Israelis have no intention of giving up or dismantling. It happens to be in the very centre of the West Bank where any future Palestinian state must be based. I remember Alex and his passion for mud baths in the Dead Sea, but we decide not to stop there.

Jericho is the most attractive town on the West Bank. It narrowly lost out to Ramallah when Arafat had to decide on the capital city of his state-to-be. When we get there it seems to be asleep. Jericho used to lure Israeli gamblers to its casino but they no longer come to lose their money. With no clients, the casino has closed, another victim of the Intifada and the fear Israel feels.

We head north. The landscape of Galilee is splendid. There are many holidaymakers round the lake at Tiberias where Jesus walked on the water. Just outside the town, the sound of bombs shakes us out of our tourist torpor. Up in the north, there is a war.

But this war is very different from the one I drove to 24 years ago. Yes, there is the sound of explosions and some pillars of smoke blackening the horizon but in 1982, when I drove north with another journalist, Bernard Cohen, we kept seeing tanks and trucks loaded with war equipment going to the border.

In the summer of 1982 the Israeli army invaded Lebanon. Most Israelis, including many on the right, *now* think that decision was either criminal or just politically wrong-headed.

In 1982 the army also had an infallible plan in its drawer.

A few months before the plan was put into action, I accompanied the newly elected French President, François Mitterand, on his first official visit to Israel. Monsieur Le President was in fine humor, his famously wry smile played on his lips as a grim and dour Menachem Begin welcomed him to the Jewish state. The state visit proceeded normally, with a busy itinerary of official engagements and lavish dinners.

Mitterand had lots of stamina, although he was already ill. We were all exhausted in the wake of the 65-year-old President.

Towards the end of an official banquet, at which the wine flowed freely, the Israelis produced a map, and explained they would have to rid Lebanon of the PLO and its leader, Arafat. It was not made explicit that disposing of Arafat would mean sending him into exile, if the plans to assassinate him did not work out. (Ariel Sharon would later publicly regret not 'liquidating' Arafat at the time.) The French diplomats at the banquet took this belligerent talk for mere chatter over cognac. They did not think it could seriously be the policy of the State of Israel.

Six months later, after a Palestinian tried to kill the Israeli ambassador to London, Begin invaded Lebanon. Only then did the French diplomats recall the end of the conversation at the state dinner.

The first Lebanon war forced the PLO to leave Beirut and move their HQ to Tunis. The hawks in Israel had beaten the doves of the Peace Now movement, which was powerful enough to get hundreds of thousands of demonstrators on the streets. The biggest protest drew over a quarter of a million people to Tel Aviv. The total population of Israel then was 5 million.

The hawks thought they had won and paid no attention to one small detail. In 1982, the Iranians, just three years after Ayatollah Khomeini's Revolution, felt that the Palestinian resistance was rather feeble. So they decided to send 1,000 revolutionary guards to Beirut to stiffen it. These Iranians wanted a name that would trumpet their devotion to Allah and called themselves 'Hez Allah', the 'Party of Allah' or 'Party of God'.

Today it is that famous brand – Hezbollah.

And that is how the great solution to the problem of 1982 has come back to bite. Psychoanalysts speak of cures that only deal with the symptoms of mental torment, without tackling the underlying cause. Such superficial cures often leave the wounds to fester – and festering wounds tend to erupt in an even more deadly form. The 1982 invasion of Lebanon prompted Iran to create Hezbollah. The Americans call such unintended consequences 'blowback'.

Hezbollah went as far as South America to execute its missions. In 1994, it perpetrated the worst terrorist act Argentina ever suffered. A suicide car bomb killed 95 people in a Jewish community centre in Buenos Aires. The kamikaze driver was a Lebanese Shiite.

Today, July 13, as we approach the Lebanese border the noise is atrocious. Explosions shake the small town of Kiryat Shmona and the frontier village of Metulla.

'How do you tell the difference between incoming rockets and outgoing Israeli artillery,' I asked my companion, a veteran war reporter, back in 1982.

'If there is a *boom* first followed by a whistling noise, it's the artillery,' he explained. 'The Katyushas whistle and land in one fell swoop. In the Second World War, their sound was so distinctive they were called the *Organs of Stalin.'*

Now it is very different from the first Lebanon war. The roads are clear. There aren't jams of tanks or heavy vehicles rolling towards the border to invade. There are just some jeeps, a few military busses and some artillery positions.

The war is being fought from the air, as the former Air Force chief, Halutz, wants it to be. Planes hurtle through the sky. Hezbollah dodges the Israeli bombs and beats its record for rockets launched every day. On the Israeli side of the border, people scurry into shelters. On the Lebanese side, they try to flee north.

From the ground, an air war is hard to follow. You hear noises – and understand nothing at all.

I also have no idea that during the night of July 14 and early morning of July 15, the Israeli army sends in more elite units to surprise Hezbollah. Yet again, the tactic doesn't work because Hezbollah refuse to understand the rules and do not run away. Hezbollah fighters attack the elite Israeli units, just one kilometer inside Lebanon.

Summer Rain

We listen to the BBC, which reports from Beirut that Israeli planes have demolished the bridges, the Al Manar television studios and petrol dumps. The Israeli army has asked the Lebanese government to evacuate the southern suburbs of Beirut where many Hezbollah followers live. Nasrallah, of course, is no longer there and has gone either to his own bunker or to Syria.

I had hoped to cross the border to talk to Israeli soldiers. But it is quite impossible. After a few hours of being deafened by artillery and explosions while, seeing nothing, we head back to Jerusalem.

July 15

In the morning the kids are glad to see *both* of their parents. They had gone to the festival and watched more depressing World War Two movies. Then they came back to the hotel and saw the news with its images of war.

Hezbollah breaks new records. For the first time they manage to hit Haifa, which is the country's main industrial and technological centre. They have also hit Tiberias which we drove through yesterday. The kids don't know Hebrew but they catch the word 'Katyusha'.

I have to flash back again.

Eight years ago, the children spent the summer at the Club Med at Arziv, ten minutes from the Lebanese border. The sun was sparkling, just like the pina coladas. No rockets disturbed the serious business of getting a tan or chatting up any talent. Sea, sex and sun.

But the Israelis warned no one that summer – or certainly not Club Med – of their plan to assassinate the then boss of Hezbollah. The thinking was the usual; if we kill the leader of the terrorists, we reduce the dangers we face.

That evening rockets fall on the Club Med paradise to avenge the death of the Hezbollah leader.

The security men at the Club are quick. They sound the alarm, push the dancers out of the disco and down into the shelters. Our kids spent the night in the shelter.

When we picked them up at dawn, they had been impressed by the coolness of the Israeli teenagers. They were singing and laughing. They weren't scared.

Club Med closed its premises at Arziv. There would be no more sex and surf.

The Israeli attack on Hezbollah's leader eight years ago had been successful but it did not eliminate the danger that the organisation posed. Hezbollah grew from strength to strength and Hassan Nazrallah became its Secretary General.

On the third and fourth day of this 'war', the Israeli press is still backing the government.

'Everything that is linked to Hezbollah must be attacked,' says *Yehodot Aharanot* which has one of the largest circulations in Israel, *'we must hit their Headquarters, their training camps, their arsenals and their bunkers and hangars.'*

'This time we must go to the end,' says *Maariv,* the other big daily here.

Haaretz, the *Guardian* of Israel, is more moderate and warns that the deployment of phenomenal force by Israel risks getting out of control and setting in motion a dangerous process of escalation, as happened in 1982.

The battle of information and misinformation has started. Then the leader of Hezbollah boasts of a triumph so spectacular that no one believes him.

'A missile has hit an Israeli warship off the coast of Beirut,' announces Nasrallah in a live interview. We are asked to believe that a warship, armed with a missile defence system, has itself been hit by a missile.

The Israeli military deny this lunatic claim. The parents of the sailors are reassured. But not for long.

The knock on the door comes during the night. Families hear the truth. The anti-missile frigate *Hanit* has indeed been hit by a missile – an Iranian one – launched from the Lebanese coast. One sailor, then two sailors, then three, then four, are missing. We understand that 'missing' means dead.

On Day 4, the bombings don't just hit the Lebanese infrastructure, but also civilians trying to flee. In the Shiite village of Zebquine, a family of some thirty people is killed on

the road. At Marwahine, Israeli forces use loud speakers
to tell the inhabitants to leave their village. The villagers try
to.

'We just had the time to run to the United Nations camp
but they would not let us in,' the villagers tell *Libération*'s
special correspondent in Lebanon. 'So we left in convoy and
took the road up into the mountains.'

The hills are no protection from air strikes. Twenty-three
civilians are killed, including many children.

'Why are we bombing the Lebanon?' a reporter asks Amir
Peretz, the Minister of Defence, who came into politics
from the Histradut, Israel's trade union federation. His background has made him an expert in pay negotiations, a man
who knows when to call a strike and when to cut a deal. But
he seems clueless as Minister of Defense. He should know the
reason for the bombing: Chief of Staff Dan Halutz does not
like the infantry. The doctrine is 'bomb them into submission!'
War is now a technological affair, as the Americans showed
in the first Gulf War and its less popular sequel, Gulf War 2.
If you hit them from the air, especially when the enemy has
no air force to speak of, you don't risk the lives of your own
men.

But Gulf War 2 is still actually being fought in the streets of
Baghdad and Basra. The Israeli copy-cats seem to be blind to
the fact that overwhelming air superiority has never won the
day by itself. Not in Vietnam, not in Iraq and not now.

And it will turn out that while busily arranging his air strikes,
Halutz has found time to ring his stockbroker and sell his
portfolio of shares. Clearly our air hero expects the Tel Aviv
Stock Exchange to crash.

Peretz leaps into the fray, but he has no experience of this
kind of thing. Many eyebrows were raised when the former
union baron was appointed Minister of Defense in Olmert's
coalition. He had campaigned on a promise to alleviate poverty
in Israel, and wanted the Ministry of Finance. Peretz has always

been close to the Peace Now movement, and is the first Mizrahi (Arab) Jew to lead a major political party. It was a clever move on Olmert's part to insist on his taking the defence portfolio, effectively neutralizing the Labour leader's ability to press for further withdrawals from the Occupied Territories. It's also damaged his standing with Labour's supporters, who want social democracy and peace from their leaders, not air raids on Beirut.

Thus trapped, Peretz turns from dove to hawk on the first day of the conflict. An old general, a hero of previous wars like Rabin might well have kept his cool, and told Halutz that air raids would only lead to massive civilian casualties, and a propaganda coup for Hezbollah. But Peretz allows himself to be convinced by the arguments deployed in military briefings. He holds the line: Lebanon is responsible for terrorist acts launched from its territory. The operation must stop Hezbollah from ever again having any access to the Israeli border.

How, exactly?

I call Mark Heller, a smart political analyst at Tel Aviv University, to help me analyse the situation for my readers who, God knows, want some analysis.

Our readers won't be disappointed.

'There is no plan. If the government had a coherent plan it's a well kept secret,' Heller snipes.

He also has suggestions for the government.

'Israel has to re-establish its image as all-powerful in the region. We need to hit them hard to discourage Hezbollah from attacking us again, and also to put pressure on the political class in the Lebanon, so that they finally do something serious about disarming the militias.'

After Heller, I ring the correspondent who follows military matters for *Yedioth* – and get the opposite point of view. Alex Frishman, like all military specialists in all papers in the world, is much more supportive of the military. He cannot imagine that his friends with epaulettes were genuinely surprised.

'Heller is wrong. There is a plan – and this plan has been in existence for a long time,' says Frishman. But the military were waiting for the government to green light it. There are three phases to this plan. 'The first phase is the air raids on the infrastructure of Lebanon. Hammer the roads, the airports, the bridges, the communication centres and the military installations of Lebanon. Phase 2 is to strike Hezbollah's centres and increase the pressure on the Lebanese government. The naval and aerial blockade are succeeding in that.'

'And Phase 3?' I ask.

'More and more pressure on the government in Beirut so that it understands it will pay a heavy price if it does not attend to the situation in the south of its country.'

Phases 1 and 2 have led the Lebanese government – which includes two members of Hezbollah – to write to the Security Council. The letter, Frishman points out, is telling, as it states for the first time that the Lebanese government has the right to insist on having its authority extend to the whole of its country. The language speaks of Lebanon for the Lebanese, not for the militias.

'Precisely what Israel is asking for?' Frishman asks.

Unfortunately Hezbollah is paying no attention to Phase 1 and 2.

You don't have to be a smart military analyst in the Israeli High Command to realise that the bombing has not smashed Hezbollah's capacity to respond.

Every day Hezbollah fires more and heavier missiles, which penetrate further into Israel, causing more damage and casualties.

In fact, the question now is: will the missiles reach as far as Tel Aviv?

Saturday evening. A friend is giving a dinner party in Tel Aviv so that we can discuss the situation. He is a wise old bird from Alexandria, who is both a psychiatrist and a diplomat. He usually exudes Jewish humour, but tonight he starts in sombre mood.

'Not very good, this story,' he says.

'You don't have confidence in the military and their political finesse?'

'You can put it that way,' he smiles enigmatically, as befits a shrink and Sphinx.

It's a beautiful night, warm and balmy. The food is a splendid Middle Eastern feast any sheikh would be proud to offer his guests. Everyone talks across everyone else – but we finally stop as someone asks the anxious question in everyone's mind.

'How far will they go?'

But does that mean Hezbollah with its 12,000 or 14,000 missiles? Or does it mean the Israeli government?

Both, we all agree.

The dinner guests – writers, journalists, musicians, shrinks – metamorphose into military experts. We discuss tactics and strategies. The only thing we don't have is a big map of the Middle East on which we could use knives, forks, salt and pepper-pots to mark who has forces where.

I imagine a similar dinner in 1915 when the Great War seemed impossible to predict because it was hard to work out whether the British, French or German generals were more incompetent: 'So, old boy, Mon General, Verdun – is it lost or won? Half lost? Half won?'

Those of us who smoke on the balcony can't help but peer into the sky – just in case a rocket is scudding across the lights of the city.

'What floor are you on in your hotel in Tel Aviv?' One smoker asks an American guest.

'The Ninth floor. Why?'

'Do you have a view of Jaffa – to the south?'

'No, I look out on the pool.'

'So you're facing north! Bad luck. You're in the line of fire from Lebanon.'

If Hezbollah aim for Tel Aviv, the missile might smash into his room – and mini bar.

It's half a joke, of course, but it hits home. The next day the man gets a plane to New York, abandoning his room, with its view of Lebanon in the far distance.

July 16

Haifa is not far from Tel Aviv. If you ignore the speed cameras you can do it in an hour.

But since last Friday, Haifa is a different world.

Ever since the 1920s, Haifa has been a symbol of possible co-existence. Jews and Arabs, Christians and Muslims have all lived here together. It is a city of dockers, traders, and researchers, based around the famous Technion Research Institute. Jews, Arabs and Christians are still together here, confined in their apartment buildings, in windowless rooms which were meticulously designed not to crumble in case of attack. In the older buildings there are shelters in the basement.

When the first rockets hit Haifa, I rang my cousin who was cool about the whole thing.

'It's nice of you to phone but everything is normal. We're going to work, doing the shopping,' she sounds almost ironic. 'There's no panic, there's nothing to report.'

A few minutes later, her voice trembles. She is locked up in the bike shed which serves as a shelter for her building – and her mother is with her.

'The most frightening thing is the wailing of the sirens which rise and fall,' she says. 'After the sirens go, all you can do is wait, wait for the noise of the blast.'

A bunch of Raad missiles have just landed on Haifa, terrorising its 275,000 inhabitants. 'We might target Haifa,' Haj Hassan, one of Hezbollah's members of Parliament, had warned but no one took the threat seriously – hardly surprising, as Israeli intelligence missed the fact that Party of God had been stock-piling rockets, anti-tank missiles, anti-aircraft batteries, and

45

rocket launchers – all in formidable quantities. Generously offered by Iran, delivered through Syria.

In 1973, when the Egyptians got their Russian SAM 7 missiles out of their cases James Bond-style, Israeli boffins had to work out counter measures. Haifa's Technion worked round the clock, the best Jewish brains in the universe were consulted, and solutions were improvised. Three days later, the Russian SAM 7 started to miss their targets. The boffins were so clever they managed to interfere with the telemetry and, even, get some SAMs to boomerang back on those who launched them.

Today there seems to be no clever scientific solution. Hezbollah are not all that high tech but they are very resourceful. They have put their rocket launchers on jeeps and drive around Lebanon firing at will.

'Hezbollah has been damaged,' Israeli spokesmen keep on repeating. But they have still managed to launch rockets from the port of Tyre. One hits the very heart of Haifa. It crashes on a hangar at the railway station. Eight men die and 17 people are injured. It's the worst incident Israel has had to deal with so far.

Judaism forbids the filming of dead bodies and the television stations will not show footage of Israeli victims. On this side of the border, all we see is a huge hole in the hangar's roof and a massive puddle of blood. This is a good way to lose the media war from the start.

The loss of life is, of course, a triumph for Hezbollah. But the Katyushas, Stalin's Organs, are old World War Two weapons and not very accurate. Hezbollah would have much preferred to hit the oil refineries in the harbour and set off a chain of explosions in the old city. Oil refinery fires always make great TV footage.

After this strike, the dangerous chemicals in the port of Haifa are moved down south.

Very fast.

The attack changes the attitude of my cool, self-possessed

cousin. Like all my family she is left-wing. She opposed the first war in Lebanon and the repression of the Palestinians in Gaza. But rockets make a difference.

'Hezbollah declared war on us. We have no choice, we can't stop,' she says, now resigned to the military solution. 'We have to push Hezbollah back from the border.'

Five days ago, when the operation began, Israel was a divided society. Four hundred rockets, twelve dead and the fear everyone feels have succeeded in healing all the divisions in Israeli society. There are no appeasers now. All Israelis support their army and their Prime Minister. In his best manly voice, Olmert says *'Israel will never give in to threats.'*

I head north to Haifa again.

The traffic jam is on the road south. Israelis are fleeing as far from the border as possible, pushing towards Tel Aviv.

In Lebanon the flow is the very opposite. Terrified civilians are heading north to Beirut to avoid bombs raining down. If they can't go north, they try going east to Syria.

As I get closer to the war zone, the motorway is empty. Silence reigns. I find the silence eerie and frightening. Haifa is usually such a bustling town. Hezbollah has had a real success here. One million people in the north of Israel can no longer live their normal lives. A third have left their houses and their jobs. Many manage a trace of their usual swagger and say they expect to be back in a day or two. Surely it can't take any longer for our boys to sort out the terrorists?

The silence is ruptured only by the sirens. I am still not scared of the incoming Katyushas because I have not adjusted to the situation. Hezbollah has not managed to knock out the traffic lights, though I figure no one is going to give me a ticket if I drive through them. I ignore every red light I meet.

Finding Haifa Railway Station is not hard: it is the only place where there is any noise. The Hebrew word for 'railway' is 'rackevet' – which I suspect comes from the English 'making a racket', which is what trains do. (In the early 1900s Hebrew

47

had to invent thousands of words which had not been needed in the Bible!) Police, ambulances, rabbis, television crews are all working; people are shouting. The dead and injured have been moved since Jews, like Muslims, have to bury their dead within 24 hours. A legacy of ancient times: better bury the bodies decently, before the desert sun starts rotting them. In Haifa, as in Beirut, families will be trying to do what their religion demands.

Fragments of the missile litter the road. There is a massive hole and the twisted metal of the missile.

It brings back to me the horrors of the Synagogue at the Rue Copernic in Paris in 1980, when a booby-trapped motor bike exploded and killed four people. And it reminds me of the bomb in a dustbin in the Rue des Rennes in Montparnassse where I saw bits of arms and legs spread across the pavement in front of a bookshop.

I walk away towards the alleyways of the old quarter called the Wadi. The streets are empty. The only people I see are an Arab family who are having coffee outside their house. What astonishing calm. They offer me a wonderful Turkish coffee.

'The mayor of Haifa is brilliant,' says Leila, the mother, who works for the city. 'He fights for everyone who lives here. He makes no distinctions whatever. Anyway we have had no problems here. Look at the streets around us. Jews live here. Arabs live here, we've always lived together but we are very nervous since the rockets started to rain down. Luckily we've managed to set up two rooms in our house where we can take shelter.'

'It's terrible that so many people are dying,' one of the kids adds in English. 'This should be resolved by diplomacy, not war. They should talk, not fight. And the Lebanese have nothing to do with this conflict.'

Then we stop abruptly. A siren wails. All the family members get up and go to their safe rooms in the house. The hit on the train station has made it obvious how dangerous the situation is. Katyushas do not distinguish between Jews and Arabs.

I get back in my car and drive to the beach. I have read an interview in *Ha'aretz* with Tony Matar, the owner of the Maxim restaurant, which is famous both for its fish and for being the target of the first terrorist attack in Haifa in October 2003. A female suicide bomber killed 21 Jews and Arabs as they ate lunch there.

Tony Matar refuses to be intimidated. All the restaurants in Haifa are closed but he announces that Maxim will stay open – even if there are no customers.

I walk down the hill and see his place. Maxim's huge windows face out on to the sea and also on to a disused railway track. When the British ruled the Middle East you could take a train from Cairo to Beirut, stopping off at Tel Aviv and Jerusalem. I wonder, in utopian mode, if I will ever be able to take that train. It would be nice.

Maxim's is empty but Tony Matar is there. He speaks perfect French, which he learned at the Christian school in Haifa.

'I'm open not because I expect any business,' Matar tells me, 'but to show that life goes on. I've spent two days at home doing sod all and I decided that I would not let myself be beaten.'

Matar is 39 years old, slim, well-dressed and looks like a modern businessman. He speaks Hebrew, as do all Israeli Arabs, as well as Arabic – and English, because it is 'the language of business'. An Israeli Arab who uses *we* in referring to Israel is a rarity in this country – and you will only meet one in Haifa.

'Every time there is an alert I get phone calls from friends, half are Jewish, the other half are Arab. I am an Israeli Arab and I am reacting to this situation like all other Israelis. If Hezbollah had not attacked that patrol and kidnapped two soldiers, there wouldn't be a war today. If we don't deal with Hezbollah once and for all, this kind of crisis will happen again and again. The world speaks of the bombs hitting the Lebanon but people are attacking us every day and no one speaks of that. I support this operation in the Lebanon totally. One day the countries of the Middle East will thank us for having rid them of the Party of God.'

No customers come to eat at Maxim's but Tony stays there until a missile lands just a few metres away. Then he closes his restaurant – and goes home.

Before driving away I manage to get through to Salah Abassi, a writer who also publishes books in Arabic.

'We the Arabs of Haifa are in the same situation as the Jews, stuck and stuffed in our houses,' he tells me on the phone. 'This town is not like in Tel Aviv or Jerusalem. The Jews and Arabs understand each other. Even the wars of 1967 and 1973 did not change the fact we have a good relationship. I will stay in Haifa whatever happens. I adore the town.'

'What do you think of the war?' I ask.

'Utterly ridiculous. On both sides. Hezbollah's kidnapping of two soldiers was absurd and the response of the Israelis, the strongest army in the region, is also absurd. Can you tell me why they are attacking Beirut?'

I splutter but have no answer.

'Come by the house, have some tea and I will show you my library and my exhibition of Hebrew and Arabic literature.'

I would love to go and talk with Salah Abassi, but it does not seem very wise to drive through this deserted town where I don't know the way too well with sirens blaring constantly. The atmosphere has made me less reckless. I promise to visit him the next time I am in Haifa and head for the motorway. But then, I change my mind. I can't leave Haifa without going to see my uncle, Marcel Greilsammer. He is 103 years and some months old and he has not joined the exodus south. Many other old people are still here, like the Arabs, the new immigrants, and foreign workers from Asia, who all have nowhere else to go. My uncle is probably the oldest person left in Haifa.

Yet again I get lost but, finally, I find his building. When I ring his bell the Philippino who looks after him lets me in. He is delighted to have a visitor. He had decided not to go down into the shelter when the sirens sounded because he did not want to leave my uncle alone.

'We decided to push his wheelchair on to the hall in the staircase,' he says in English, 'because it's too hard to get it down into the shelter.'

I inspect the hall and agree. There are no windows. It's nearly as good as the shelter.

My uncle is looking at Fox News which is showing pictures of the shattered hangar of the railway station and of the police and emergency services. Uncle is following the story with total attention.

'You're not scared with all these sirens,' I say as I sit down by him.

'No,' he replies in his croaky voice, 'it is not that frightening and it is certainly far less frightening than the First World War.'

He was born in 1902 and was twelve when the Great War started. For him that remains the only true war. But he concedes that, 'the sirens are annoying'.

He's right of course. Compared to the 20 million who died in 1914–1918, this is a tiny war. But it has still managed to paralyse a third of the country.

This may be the last time I get to see my uncle and so, when he wants to talk about the past, we talk about the past. It has been 86 years since he graduated from high school.

'You got a grade Excellent, like my father did,' I say. 'You were brilliant students too but after that, it skipped a generation, mine...'

He laughs and remembers how well he did in the competition to enter France's prestigious School of Mining. He is he oldest surviving member of the School and remembers it with great affection.

My uncle always provides a moral tonic. He has chronically good humour, which has allowed him to survive all the

51

vicissitudes of the 20th century, the century that holds the record for massacres and human cruelties. That good humour must have helped when he organized services for Yom Kippur as a prisoner of war. As a French officer, he was not sent to a concentration camp but treated as a POW. Ironically, my uncle survived for five years because the Vichy government persuaded the Nazis to treat all French prisoners of war correctly. Any Jews in the army were treated properly, at the start at least.

Uncle's good humour helped when he learned how to drive at the age of 48, and when, at the age of 84, he decided to move to Israel. When he got here, he plunged right in and started to learn Hebrew in classes with kids who had just arrived from Russia and Ethiopia.

His life journey has been extraordinary – from the Alsace to Haifa. He has always loved classical culture and is a Jewish humanist. For twenty years, he served as president of the synagogue in Rue Copernic which was bombed, and, as far as I can judge, he is still what he has always been – a true Parisian.

'I am sorry I can't go to Paris any more,' he told me sadly when he neared his 100th birthday. It was only then that he felt too frail to take his annual trip to the city of his childhood, which always included a journey in the metro.

Talking to him reassures me; he is clearly well for a man of his age. I wonder if I could drive him to Tel Aviv or Jerusalem but it seems impossible and, anyway, he shows no signs of wanting to leave. I kiss him, thinking that it might be for the very last time.

I am supposed to file a story – and I have a good one. *'Haifa the ghost town'* or *'Missiles don't notice if you're Arabic or Jewish'*. But unlike the TV reporters, I don't have a satellite link, so I have to look for an Internet Café. Everything is closed. I have no alternative but to hurry to Tel Aviv to file.

I turn on the radio. The toll of dead and injured is increasing. Beirut airport has been bombed again. Embassies are evacuating their nationals. The Lebanese Red Cross reports at least 140 dead. On this side of the border, rockets have hit Safed and Haifa. The Israeli army is still performing poorly. It has failed to take a Hezbollah base four kilometers inside Lebanon and sustained major losses in the attempt. But there is one success. The military claim to have brought down a missile – made in Iran – which was headed for Tel Aviv.

The lack of military triumph only makes Olmert's government more stubborn. 'We will continue our offensive and we do not negotiate with terrorists,' Jerusalem insists.

Olmert is dealing with a better poker player, I fear. The Secretary General of Hezbollah, Nasrullah, teases Israel, promising the country 'more surprises'. He doesn't bother to add that they will be unpleasant ones,

What no one knows till much later is that the war could have stopped that day. On July 16, the Israeli Foreign Minister finally manages to speak to her Prime Minister, who has been avoiding her. Tzipi Livni is an attractive and determined woman. Since the very start, she has had a diplomatic solution, but the Prime Minister with the military inferiority complex has cancelled all their meetings. He has been too busy to see her because he has had to confer constantly with his generals, real men.

The Foreign Office has been skeptical of the military solution from the beginning. Its view is that bombing Lebanon will not make Hezbollah release the two soldiers.

When Livni finally gets to see Olmert, she tells him that she and her ministry have simple and sensible diplomatic solutions. 'We need to mobilize the international community so that it sends a proper force to Lebanon and imposes an embargo on arms sales to Hezbollah,' she insists.

Olmert will have none of it. He replies there is no question of allowing an international force. Israel will fight until it frees its kidnapped soldiers.

Livni is astonished and silent. She is the Foreign Minister and she understands this war is going nowhere. Yet she has been sidelined, while the none-too-successful military get their way.

It is very ironic. I can't help thinking that if there were one war hero in the cabinet, one general who had fought a successful campaign, today's less than brilliant generals would be given their marching orders. As Clausewitz said, war is far too important to be left to generals.

July 17

I get yet another e-mail from another hysterical reader after my article appears on *Libération*'s website.

Hysteric 2 complains about my interview with Tony Matar, the restaurant owner.

'How dare you steal a piece from Ha'aretz. It is rotten journalism but it does not surprise me at all,' says Hysteric 2.

I wonder whether he is not surprised because of me – personal lack of ethics – or because of *Libération* – company lack of ethics – or because of French journalists – national lack of ethics – or because of journalists in general – total lack of ethics.

'I've been perfectly ethical,' I reply. 'I did go and see Tony Matar in his restaurant and spoke to him, I did not pirate my piece from *Ha'aretz*.'

Hysteric 2 does not believe me, of course.

'You wrote the same article. Matar said the same thing in the Israeli papers.'

'Did no one ever tell you,' I reply, 'that two different journalists can interview the same person and he can say the same thing to both of them? In fact that would be normal. I begin to find your accusations insulting. I have his mobile number if you want to check that I've met him.'

Bad mistake. I couldn't have found a better way of proving my lack of ethics as far as my accuser is concerned.

'So you're ready to give me his number. You have no principles whatever.'

I give up. I put his e-mail address on my blocked list.

The war also leads to commercial collateral damage. The hotels in Tel Aviv are empty. With our magic surfboard, we are the only paying customers. The Americans have gone – or else they never came. Most travel plans involving Israel have been cancelled. Only a few frummers, the ultra Orthodox Jews of the Midwest and Brooklyn, can still be seen in Jerusalem, their women in long modest dresses and the men crowned with skullcaps. But English is no longer heard much on the beach.

With rockets being fired and airplanes flying overhead, most Americans have no wish to explore this unknown territory.

Another casualty of war is the bar mitzvah industry. My friend David, who books hotel rooms and apartments for visitors, is very upset by his clients' lack of consideration.

'They have cancelled a bar mitzvah with 300 guests,' he laments.

'You'll fill the hotel and the flats with refugees from the north,' I try to console him. 'They're starting to come.'

'But even if they do come, they won't pay the same prices. The refugees are heading for Eilat or will camp in the desert. They won't be booking the deluxe suites.'

But many hotels then amaze us with a patriotic gesture. They offer generous discounts: some true Samaritans even pay for free accommodation for the *People from the North*, a new and disadvantaged social class in Israeli society.

The People from the North remind me of those who fled New Orleans in the wake of Hurricane Katrina. I saw them arrive in Los Angeles, where they were well received in one of the capitals of world capitalism. The kids were given mountains of toys, hairdressers gave free hairdos, others found jobs for the young people. The University of California offered free tuition to displaced students. The stars of the Lakers, the famous basketball team, took them out for dinner.

Everyone in Los Angeles did what they could to help. The same cannot be said of the Bush administration. Washington has washed its hands. The People from the North in Israel are being treated just as generously by the State. The government is doing nothing for them. But the Home Front, as Ehud Olmert calls it, does not break. And for once he has evidence for his soundbite.

The pollsters have been at work, asking Israelis. *'Are you for or against the operation?*

The question is put to a representative sample of the whole Israeli population – Jews, Arabs, Druze and Christians. Eighty-one per cent say 'yes' – and Israel is one of the most divided and factionalised societies on earth. The Knesset has 120 members from twelve separate political parties (many of which are themselves coalitions of even smaller factions, such as Labour-Meimad and Meretz-Yachad). Now only a very small minority – made up of Israeli Arabs and left-wing Jews – want the fighting stopped and insist that there should be negotiations.

To discuss the polls, I phone Daniel Bensimon, the political analyst of *Ha'aretz.*

'This is nothing new,' he says. 'First, Israelis are always very united at the start of the war and being under fire does produce solidarity. Then Israelis are ready to sacrifice their summer so that future summers will be calmer.'

You will remember most people were ready to sleep with Arafat to bring peace.

But Bensimon adds that the fate of Olmert depends on how the war goes. 'If the war ends with some sort of movement towards peace, Olmert will have won, but otherwise...'

The Prime Minister already has his Six Days War – the country has been at war for that long now. He has the support of his population and even of moderate Arab countries. He would even have the support of the Lebanese if he were not bombing them. Everyone will be rather pleased if he manages to get rid of Hezbollah extremists or weakens them. Olmert even has the support of the pacifists of Peace Now and writers like David Grossman, an advocate of a just peace between Israel and the Palestinians.

Summer Rain

In an article written for *Libération*, David Grossman argues: *'Today this war is legitimate. Israel attacks Lebanon because that country is an official ally of Hezbollah and because Israel is being bombed from that country. Everyone knows that Hezbollah is a creature of Iran and that its whole purpose is to destroy the state of Israel. The relationship between the Palestinians and Israel is completely different; these two peoples have to find a way of resolving their differences if they want to keep living in this region.'*

I look in my address book because I want to contact other well-known pacifists to see if they too are supporting the war. Yossi Beilin was one of the key negotiators of the Oslo Agreement and, later, a signatory of the unofficial Geneva Peace Accord with the Palestinians in 2003. He is now leader of the left-wing Meretz-Yachad coalition, the most dovish of all Zionist parties, which makes him, if only by default, the leader of the opposition on the left. He does not respond to my many phone calls. But to the Israeli press he offers a careful and subtle, if somewhat vague, message: 'This operation is legitimate as long as the methods do not contradict fixed objectives.'

Which means would contradict which objectives, he does not say specifically.

Roy Yellin, the spokesman for Beilin's party Meretz, does call me back, and is much clearer.

'The rockets are falling on the villages of Galilee and Haifa where a large part of the population is Arab. It is the duty of the state to defend its citizens. A country has the right to defend itself. The question is one of knowing how far we go. The military option will not be enough. We will need a negotiated ceasefire.'

I feel I have done my job and listened to the voices of the Israeli left, the voices European liberals love so much. Then I go back to meet Itamar, a genial filmmaker whose politics are anarcho-artistic.

Itamar is sitting in a plastic chair which he has put right in the sea. The waves lap around him. I take another chair and dangle my legs in the ocean very happily. The water is a bit dirty this late in the day, but shellfish flirt with us and it's magical, drinking beer and watching the sun set on Tel Aviv.

'You might be called up as a reservist,' I say to Itamar. 'You're not so old.'

'No chance,' he laughs at me and produces a big joint, as usual. Drugs are at least as common in Israel as in Britain and the US.

'The last time I was in the army was in Lebanon in 1983,' he says. 'I was stuck in the kitchen baking cakes and they refused to take me on any night commando operation.'

I asked Itamar to explain this calamity.

'Because of my political views,' Itamar asked his commander.

'No, because you can't shoot straight. If I let you shoot you're as likely to shoot me as any enemy.'

'What were you doing in Lebanon in 1983?' I ask Itamar.

'I wish I knew. One day a general came to give us a talk. He explained that we were to attack a Shiite village. No one asked any questions. Only me. I asked why are we attacking the Shiites. The villagers are not our enemies.'

This question bothered Itamar's commander who made the position clear to the visiting general. He said: 'General, this soldier is the cook and confined to the kitchen. The most lethal weapon we will put in his hand is a vegetable knife. He's going nowhere near any fighting.'

So the army attacked the village and Itamar attacked the aubergines.

He laughs as he finishes his *Soldier Schweik* tale and orders another beer.

We sip, calm and companionable. Many beers later as the sun is going down Itamar says something that amazes me.

'I live in Tel Aviv. I can imagine and accept that they fling one or two missiles in our direction. It's a big town. The likelihood that the missiles will hurt me or my family is small.

Okay. But a nuclear attack by Iran, that's more of a problem. So I think about that and finally I think bombing Teheran as a precaution would be quite cool.'

July 18

And on the Seventh Day The Lord God, Lord of Hosts, rested, if you believe Genesis. He had been worn out by his self-imposed task of creation.

The Israeli General Staff does not rest, but, nor does it create. It destroys from on high and claims to have wiped out one third of Hezbollah's arsenal of rockets. The estimate is that the Party of God has 12,000 missiles, so now they are down to 8,000. The war should be over in 14 more days, assuming they fire off their rockets at the same rate. Israel also claims to have destroyed the road from Damascus on which the arms are being delivered.

The army is over-optimistic yet again. After the war, Hassan Nasrallah will come out of hiding and address – from behind a bullet-proof screen – a crowd, which has come to celebrate his 'God given victory'. Nasrallah must like gameshows because he can behave a little like a compère on a variety show. He insists that Hezbollah is not short of weapons.

'During the war I said we had 11,000 rockets,' he crows, 'but we had more than that, we had ...'

'We had 12,000,' the crowd shouts back.

'More than that. Keep going.'

'13,000,' shouts the crowd.

Nasrallah smiles – like a good TV host.

'Stop counting. We had not even started to re-stock and we had 20,000 weapons. And we will never hand these weapons back.'

In this address, Nasrallah also used an old form of words that was hardly conciliatory: 'We must recover Palestine from the ocean to the river,' he says.

The river is the Jordan and the ocean is the Mediterranean
– and if Palestine extends over all that territory, Israel will have
been wiped out.

But on the Seventh day, Israeli public opinion is still confident
and firm. It backs a heavy military response. To make a point:
that the lives of our soldiers must not be trifled with, and we
will not tolerate any more rockets. But there are no significant
infantry moves across the border – just a few commandos
infiltrating for a few miles. Halutz still insists that the war
should be fought from afar and on high, as that is less dangerous
for our soldiers though, of course, more dangerous for Lebanese
civilians. Bombs dispatched from 5,000 metres high aren't as
pinpoint accurate as the promotional videos made by arms
manufacturers suggest.

Civilians continue to be killed on both sides. Thirteen Israelis
die from Hezbollah rockets, while 240 Lebanese, both civilians
and militia, are slain by Israeli. On the whole the international
community and the moderate Arab countries do not protest
too loudly: they are not that sorry to see Hezbollah wounded.

My editor-in-chief wants me to cover every aspect of the war
but the trouble is that I cannot find any new angle. All the
specialists, the analysts and political commentators, are re-
hashing what they said 24 or 48 hours ago. I finally convince
my editors in Paris that we have two options. Either we take
a break ourselves, because I am afraid that our readers will
succumb to Middle East news fatigue, that strange state of
mind where the most liberal of news consumers no longer care
what happens in Gaza, Jerusalem or Addis Ababa. Or they
agree to send me to the front line. I might, I don't promise,
but I might be able to get myself embedded with the commandos
who are slipping into Lebanon at night.

'Isn't it a bit dangerous ... *for a woman?*' my editor asks. I
am amazed to hear this after all these years.

'Oh yes,' I trill ironically. 'A man without a helmet is of
course more of a target than a woman with a helmet.'

July 18

'You have a helmet?' Paris asks.

'Eh, no.'

After being annoyed for 5 minutes I explain to my editor that you can rent a helmet and a bullet-proof vest. They cost 20 dollars. But I know that I will not get embedded. The Israeli military media machine is mainly organizing what we call *tourist trips* to the border, and I have already been on that particular tour. They're giving priority to television crews who need dramatic images – especially the distant blare of guns firing and, most of all, the sound of bombing: *'Live from the Israel-Lebanon border...'* It seems the Israelis want to give an adrenalin rush to the correspondents and VIPs who have come here to breathe the whiff of war.

The military have not yet taken one journalist, male or female, across the border

'I am going to try to talk to commandos as soon as they get back from their missions,' I tell my stoic colleagues in Paris, 'these missions were meant to take a few hours but they have been gone for some days. We just know that there are lots of dead and lots of wounded. The commandos have not come back yet.'

My colleague on the other side of the border, *Libération*'s special correspondent, describes a southern Lebanon that has been brought to a complete stand still. It is cut off from the rest of the country. Men women and children are trying to flee but the roads have been bombed and the bridges destroyed. They are seeing the start of a human catastrophe.

And Hezbollah?

'Hezbollah is nowhere,' he writes. *'And everywhere.'*

The Dead Sea showing the distance to Jerusalem

July 19

Alex is morally and professionally exhausted by the first week of the war, as are all the press. He has been on duty day and night. On his day off, he persuades me to go with him to his spa cure which is free and open to the public.

'A good soak in a mud bath in the Dead Sea and you'll be in perfect shape to cope with what comes next. This war won't finish in a few days,' he warns. 'It's not possible to predict how things will develop, especially as our government seems to be going nowhere, because they're listening to the military.'

I feel guilty. Taking mud baths seems like abandoning my duty. Did they take mud baths during World War Two?

'What if we did it at the end of the afternoon,' I suggest so I can stay on call during the day.

'No, I go in the morning. We're in Palestinian territory, remember, and you don't drive there during the night if you can avoid it.'

I have forgotten that Jericho is no longer that most romantic of towns, the oldest city of civilisation, where we used to go have lunch as a family. Jericho is not as tense as Nablus or Hebron, but Palestine is not a normal place to go and relax.

Nevertheless, I suggest to the kids that they come and dip in the Dead Sea with us. As we drive through the austere desert, Alex lets slip; 'We're going to the nudist beach.'

At the back of the car there is teenage uproar.

'No way. We don't want to get our clothes off before you oldies. And we don't want to see you naked either.'

'It makes no difference,' I say to quell the teenage rebellion. 'You'll be covered with mud from head to toe so no one can see whether you're wearing a bathing suit. The mud bath has been recommended since Biblical times for acne and other skin diseases, People from all over the world come to the Dead Sea because of the sea, the salt and the minerals.'

'Disgusting,' the teenagers grunt.

We pass the sign that says *Sea Level* and drive down. The Dead Sea sparkles in the red mountains of the desert. The caves of Qumran, where they found the Dead Sea Scrolls, are close by.

Floating in the salt of this ancient ocean between Jordan and Israel is healing. Alex is smart to come here every week to recover from the anxieties of the Middle East. Perhaps the next peace conference should be held here, with all the participants floating in the brine.

As we bathe, Alex and I remember a swim on the beach at Gaza many years ago.

We had gone to interview the Mayor of Gaza City. Before the Intifada, Gaza had the charm of an Egyptian seaside town. The Mayor welcomed us to his swish villa and we spoke of the day when a million people would live in Gaza. That seemed a very distant prospect then. Today, more than a million people are crammed into its tiny territory, the most densely populated place on earth.

Our dip in the Dead Sea is a kind of religious ritual even if we are nude. The modern world fades into nothing. No radio, no internet, no phone network, this is a place of unimaginable age and unimaginable peace.

The world does not let us relax long. It starts to worry that what seemed a small operation which should have crushed Hezbollah fast and given Iran a bloody nose in the process, shows no sign of being completed soon.

The Americans, Israel's most faithful ally, who never question her actions, are starting to get worked up about so-called 'collateral damage'.

'We are trying very hard to minimise the effect of the conflict on the Lebanese people,' states Condoleezza Rice, the US Secretary of State. King Abdullah of Jordan, a faithful ally of the United States, rings her to insist she must impose an immediate ceasefire.

On Monday, Dominique de Villepin, the French Prime Minister who acted so coolly in the debate at the United Nations about Saddam's Weapons of Mass Delusion, arrives in Beirut for the benefit of the cameras. He hopes that a quick trip will give him a boost in the polls. He proposes a truce and suggests that Israel stops bombing to allow humanitarian aid in.

The figures the Lebanese government publish show how this Operation has become a human catastrophe. 300 are dead, 1,000 are injured, and half a million people have been displaced. How many of these casualties were members of Hezbollah? It's impossible to know. The questions remain. Where is Hezbollah? Who is it?

'No militia man reveals himself, not even the most obscure foot soldier. Israel is waging war against an army of phantoms and shadows. You can't see them and you can't destroy them,' says Jean-Pierre Perrin, *Libération*'s special correspondent in southern Lebanon. 'Israel deploys its jets against this hidden enemy but all the planes can do is strafe anything that moves, hoping to cut Hezbollah's supply lines. The result is that the roads of south Lebanon have become a nightmare.'

Meanwhile Hezbollah's 'phantom' army launches very real rockets. As ever, rockets don't recognize differences between Arabs and Jews. A few meters from the shelter they were running to, Ravbia Taluzi and her brother Mahmoud, are killed. She was three years old; he was seven; they lived in Christ's hometown of Nazareth. Hezbollah has now managed to hit it with a missile. A true first.

The old town of Safed comes under rocket fire again. The army dispatches a commando unit to take out the Hezbollah bunker that they have identified as the launch pad for this assault. The commandos include two 21-year-old men who come from a kibbutz; they have nearly finished their military service. The unit falls into an ambush; the two 21-year-olds are killed and the army has to evacuate many wounded soldiers under Hezbollah fire.

After eight days there is something we have not seen in Israel before – doubt. Zeev Schiff, the country's leading military commentator, provides analysis every day on the army's plans and the objectives. Today he changes his tune:

'*Things are more complicated,*' we read, with some surprise, from his infallible word processor. '*The air force will not be able to deal with the problem of the missiles just by itself.*'

'Wings' Halutz, the Chief of Staff, has an explanation. It is all the fault of the enemy. 'Hezbollah want to drag Israel into a long war,' he explains to the members of the Cabinet. Who are, I assume, amazed.

A normal general – indeed a normal person – would conclude that if the enemy wants a long war, we would want a short one. Wrong, as wrong as you can get. 'We are not going to be impressed by such arguments,' says the non-military government with gigantic balls.

'Take as much time as you need to finish the job,' orders Olmert, the Prime Minister.

We are also blessed with wise words from the Minister of Defence, who had been a dove all his life, until nine days ago, but who now exudes machismo. His moustache helps, as it makes him look a little like a Mexican bandit, or Zapatista freedom fighter.

'We will not let a terrorist organization think that we're afraid of anything,' Zapata Peretz Bandito announces. This does not sound credible, coming from a man better known for threatening strike action than bombing raids. Peretz has not yet learned how to rattle his sabre.

The government sounds less and less convincing.

The daily *Yedioth Ahanoroth*, which backed the government 100% and even at times urged a more aggressive policy, starts to fret in its editorial: *'Israel has managed to score some points and has made it clear it is not to be attacked with impunity but this risks being a bitter victory.'*

July 20

The phone rings every morning.

The paper wants to know what I intend to write. Editorial explains why it cut the piece I sent yesterday – there was no space, it's summer, the news from Lebanon is more important, partly because there are more dead there. A good Israeli PR man would make sure more Jews were killed.

'Don't be upset,' Paris tries to soothe. 'On our web site we have published every word you wrote.' *Libération* has its own tensions. 'There has been lots of reaction to your piece.'

'I know, I've received lots of abusive e-mails. I'm reassured as many Jews as Arabs hate my articles. It's a good sign.'

'Yes, it's because we are very balanced in our coverage,' says the foreign news editor, with impeccable British humour.

'And is our great work as reporters helping sell the paper?'

'Absolutely not.'

That lifts my spirits.

'It's really worth running the risk of being hit on the nose by a Katyusha or being the victim of friendly fire if people don't even read the paper?'

'Your point,' says Editorial.

I ask the editor to let me go to the front.

'Why not? Go, and we'll see. If you find something interesting we'll run your piece.'

Gee, thanks.

The orchestra played on while the Titanic sank, so why shouldn't I continue my work as a correspondent at the front? I ring Oliver, the spokesman for the army, to fix a meeting on the border.

'You need a helmet and a bullet proof vest,' he says.

'I know.'

The phone keeps on pinging. Friends in Paris are worried about us.

'You're staying? Till when?' asks my friend Roland every morning. 'Why don't you come back? And the kids? Where are the kids?'

'The kids have gone to dive in the Red Sea. They want to see coral reefs, not rockets. But I'm headed North, hoping that, finally, I'll get to talk to the soldiers.'

'I am going to write an analysis of the situation to publish in a newspaper,' Roland says solemnly.

'You should wait a bit. Even the Israelis don't know what to think.'

'Ah ... And what do you think?'

'It sounds bad. But maybe I'm wrong. Meanwhile every one has forgotten the kidnapped soldiers,' I tell Roland. 'And what's the mood like in Paris?'

'Hysterical, anti-Israeli, but only in the last few days. At first people understood they had to attack Hezbollah.'

'It'll be a pity if the story ends with Hezbollah as the heroes, with Nasrallah as Robin Hood and his Iranian buddy, Mahmoud Ahmadinejad as good King Arthur firing off their little arrows against the big bad tanks. I guess we'll see. And meanwhile don't worry too much about us. It's summer and the weather is great.'

'I want to come to Israel, but I can't right now,' says Roland.

He is one of many who can't manage a visit. The Americans don't hesitate to offer advice from New York or Washington. Lots of Parisians would drop by but the war has come at a bad time for them personally. They have plans. If they had not booked that holiday in Greece, if they were not running for President, if they had not paid a deposit on that Croatian villa, if their children were not too young to leave, if the au pair hadn't run off with the best friend.

Those who don't come to Israel – too dangerous, too politically incorrect, can't find a seat on the plane – claim to support Lebanon. But they don't go to Beirut, either.

The brave few who do come realise the moment they arrive that this is not a border skirmish. This is the first round of a serious war in which Syria and Iran are starting to attack Israel and the United States. They realise that the Lebanese are the poor saps in the middle and that Hezbollah are very willing puppets. It is a new episode in the war of Islam against the evil West. Europe needs to take a stand and the international community should put this brush fire out.

Hezbollah versus Israel: the rehearsal, the test run for wars to come.

But then finally they do come. French intellectuals fly in, led by Bernard-Henri Lévy, the star of Parisian thinkers, who is the author of a book on the murder of the American journalist Daniel Pearl. Levy has always been first on the front lines in the fight against totalitarian regimes from Sarajevo to Darfur. Film makers, writers, artists, from all over the world fly in. So do war reporters who were in Sarajevo, in Baghdad, in Darfur, in New Orleans when the floods came and there was no Noah. They have decided it is worth the risk and the effort.

If a hack has given up his or her sacred summer holidays, only one thing will justify the sacrifice. Getting up to the front, being in the thick of the action – a scoop would be good – and reporting live on the events. Jil has given up her holiday and 'forgotten' her three kids at home in pursuit of these noble aims. She rings me:

'I read your piece in the plane. I said to myself. She's still there. And I'm here.'

'Where?'

'At the airport. For my radio station.'

'Well, I'm going north tomorrow. Come with me. It'll be more fun – two girls at on the front line.'

In Bernard Shaw's *Arms and the Man*, his wonderful antihero, Bluntschli (who supplies all the armies with bullets and blankets) says that what soldiers need most is chocolate – for energy and to boost their courage. We follow his advice. When we start for Haifa at dawn we take sweets. As we are diet conscious, the sweets have no sugar content. But they're still sweets, nonetheless.

July 21

After the first missile we should have kept to our plan to make for the border. Haifa comes under heavy attack. The Katyushas keep on falling.

We are in the old city, talking to people on the street and trying not to slip on the bloody ball bearings and broken glass which are everywhere. Then we hear another violent explosion.

'Where did it hit?'

'A building on Leon Blum Street,' a paramedic tells me, his phone glued to his ear.

'I can't believe it, poor bloody Leon, got by Teheran. We'd better see the damage.'

Leon Blum was the socialist Prime Minister of pre-war France, deposed, arrested and deported by the Nazis. He somehow survived the war only to be hit symbolically by the new star of anti-semitism, Mahmoud Ahmadinejad.

Jil finishes her usual live report with explosions on the soundtrack and gets into the car.

We don't need our Hebrew map. We just follow the ambulances and fire trucks, which are all heading for Leon Blum Street.

'The nuances of war matter,' I reflect to Jil, as I drive. The Japanese-sounding general, Ido Nehustan, does not speak any more of *destroying* Hezbollah but of *damaging* them and 'reducing their capability'. The war aim has been downgraded from eradicating the enemy to shrinking it.

Leon Blum Street is on a hill. The modern building which has been hit faces the Lebanon. The paranoid American who returned to New York after realising his hotel room faced north was perhaps not so paranoid, after all.

75

We climb seven or eight flights of stairs in pitch darkness. The higher we go, the more the building is wrecked. The roof gapes to the sky. The missile went through it and more or less destroyed the three floors beneath. Though the hole is impressive, no one has died. But a few people have been hurt and are in a state of shock.

'Those who stayed in the shelters were not hurt,' Ehud Olmert will boast later, when he is accused of slipping up by not evacuating the north.

Quite so – if people can manage to hold out and not go mad in these sweltering, unhealthy shelters for three or four weeks. And if they don't live in the Arab villages of the Galilee, where very little has been spent on building such shelters.

I file a piece which is very atmospheric. But I'm carried away by what I have seen at Leon Blum and forget the censorship rules. I give the exact address of the building which was hit. I have broken the rules. The militias of the Party of God read the Israeli press and watch TV news. If they pick up *Libération*, they will discover exactly how accurate their hit was – so my dispatch will help them adjust their sights next time they fire. But do they have time to read the French press?

The army spokesman, Oliver, had told us to be at a kibbutz two hours from Haifa, close to the Lebanese border and in firing range of Syria, too. We are still far from the famous Sheebaa farms. If I was the Israeli government I would have returned them long ago, as they give Hezbollah the perfect pretext to justify its armed 'resistance'.

As I drive I realise we've made slow progress.

'I think we're going to be too late, we'll only get to the front at night,' I tell my 'team'. 'That's not so smart.'

'Let's try,' Jil says. She never likes the idea of turning back.

'We don't know the area, we don't actually have the body armour and helmets.' Worse still, we seem to have been abandoned by Oliver, the army spokesman, who no longer answers his mobile phone.

July 21

'I have a bad feeling about this,' says Jil.

Our democratic forum is rudely interrupted by a wailing siren. I stop dead in the middle of the road and we leap out of the car as the Civil Defence rules tell us to do. The road runs alongside a kind of a park. There is no 'safe' stairwell or any form of shelter here, only thin tree shrubs.

Disciplined girls, the blonde and the brunette crawl into a small trench by the side of the road. The vegetation provides absolutely no protection against incoming missiles. Close to us is a couple with a small girl who have followed the same ridiculous Civil Defence rules.

The long 60 seconds pass. We pick our way out of the shrubs. The missiles did not get us but the thorns did.

Jil runs to the car to bring some of our sweets for the girl.

'She was terrified, poor girl, and she needs some candy,' explains my intrepid reporter colleague who suddenly remembers that she has three children in Paris.

'These sweets don't contain sugar since we are on a diet.'

'Never mind, it's a transitional object,' says Jil, who studied psychology before going into radio.

For the benefit of those who don't have a detailed knowledge of psychobabble and are not totally familiar with the work of D.W. Winnicott, he was an English psychoanalyst who devised the idea of 'good enough' parenting and believed kids needed transitional objects to ward off anxiety. He meant teddy bears and blankets, which small children cuddled for comfort. The Freudian consequences of eating your transitional object I dare not imagine.

We aren't ready to return to Tel Aviv so we make for the coast, which we follow all the way to the border with Lebanon.

On the tenth day the war cost even more lives. 33 people died in Israel and 338 in Lebanon.

The war is surprising even battle-hardened war reporters like Christopher Anderson, a war photographer?, who is reporting from Lebanon. He says: *'This war is not like other wars, you don't*

*see it, you only hear it and can record the victims and the destruction.
Hezbollah is invisible, a phantom. And you are followed by the noise
of drones. Here they say it is like Dresden or Chechnya; villages are
razed. But it feels like a virtual war, a video game war and the result
is that you feel even more of a target.'*

The Israeli military continues its air strikes but changes tactics
a bit. Elite soldiers cross the border on foot to try to find and
destroy the bunkers from which the rockets are being launched.
The hand-to-hand fighting is very fierce. The Israelis lose 19
men and no one knows how many Hezbollah fighters have
been killed. The Israeli soldiers bring back thirteen enemy
bodies, to be bartered for their own dead at a later stage.

Hezbollah is clearly far from being destroyed, but is it, as
the Israeli military claim, even damaged?

The head of Hezbollah is not damaged, however, but in fine
fettle. He summons a journalist from *Al Jazeera* for an exclusive
interview, which is broadcast in prime time. It takes place in
a secret location. Nasrallah knows he would make himself an
easy target if he were to go out live because Israeli satellites
would locate him in a few seconds and, very soon, he would
have a squadron of F16s on top of him.

As all too usual, the Israelis think that they will solve the
problem by eliminating the terrorist boss. They killed the
previous Secretary General of Hezbollah in 1992. Sayyed Abbas
Musawi was shot by a helicopter gunship in an attack which
also killed his wife and child. We know the result. Hezbollah
found an even smarter leader.

Very much alive and pleased with himself, Nasrallah speaks
from his hiding place. 'The Israelis are lying when they say
they have knocked out half our missiles,' he says, smiling at
the camera. 'Our message to the Zionist entity is that this war
is just beginning and our fighters can resist for a long time
and prepare more *surprises* for you.'

The Israeli army starts to call up reservists – there are 480,000
on stand-by. They leave their offices, their law practices, their

surgeries, their factories, their universities and kibbutzim. The army reckons that it takes one week to make a white collar worker fighting fit if he is over 30 years old – given that the average man drinks too much alcohol, eats too much and does not go jogging every morning. But in a week he will be transformed into a Lion of Judah who can lug 40 kilos on his back, march through the night and sneak up on six terrorists with his trusty bayonet.

This transformation takes just one week?

One of the bizarre facts of life in Israel is that prominent people are called up for active duty. In a British context imagine the unfortunate general who suddenly found that the men under his command included Jeremy Paxman and Jonathan Ross. It happens here. In normal life, Tsvika runs one of Israel's TV stations. He is called up for active duty.

'I was not in good physical shape,' he tells me. After three days of fighting he is shaken. I am not the only person who does not have a helmet and a bullet proof vest; ironically, there are not enough for the troops, which shows appalling management: you can buy them in Army Surplus shops in Tel Aviv.

Tsvika bought his own equipment before going into battle. So did many of his friends.

The army's lack of preparedness will cause many casualties.

We are getting close to real war and Jil and I hear it. The noise is terrible. Shots cross in the sky. The missiles fly south to Israel and the artillery shells fly north to Lebanon.

After we leave the resort of Nahariya – one of Hezbollah's favourite targets – which is now empty, the narrow road goes up to kibbutz Hanita, built on the border. Then the road stops. Beyond is Lebanon.

Shells fall all the time. The countryside is black, the fields are burning, and there is not one vehicle in sight. It is awesome and terrifying but, at kibbutz Hanita, everyone is calm; they're used to emergencies.

The kibbutzims are amazed and impressed to find two French

girls have turned up at the end of their road. One of the old timers, Tsvi Coriat, greets us warmly and finds us a cold beer. As he looks out from his porch, Tsvi has a splendid view of the artillery and missiles as they whirr and whiz across the sky. The end of his garden is marked by barbed wire; army jeeps sweep around the bottom of the road. We have reached the border.

Tsvi invites some other members of the kibbutz to have a drink on the terrace. Jil and I shudder at every explosion but Tsvi stays as calm as the proverbial cucumber. He discusses the media and the future of the press in France. In between the whine and whistle of two rockets, he comments on controversies which are going on in Paris. He is well-informed thanks to the web.

'We are lucky to be on this hill,' he points out. 'The missiles fly over the kibbutz and land further along in the valley.' The valley of death as the Psalmist put it.

I ring the paper and explain to my editors exactly where I am on the border. Then a missile screeches above my head. It gives me total credibility. I can confirm that the Katyushas are landing in the valley a few kilometres into Israel.

I hold my mobile away from my ear and towards the shattering explosion so that Paris can get the full of blast of sound.

'You can hear the explosion,' I say to impress them.

'Yes, yes, how *many* words are you filing?'

I seem to have got their interest now.

Tsvi comes to fetch me. 'You don't go strolling on the border,' he says. So I make my way back to the relative safety of the terrace.

'All the children have been evacuated,' a woman explains. She is a psychologist. 'I have stayed but I can't go to work. You can't drive on the roads and, anyway, all my patients have gone.'

Our hosts left Europe long ago to build a young country. They were Zionists and socialists. They have no intention of moving from their homes.

'You know you have a cousin here,' says Tsvi, out of the blue.

'Impossible, I never had a cousin in a kibbutz.'

'Yes, Nathan says you're related and he wants to see you.'

While Jil does her stuff, recording a goodly number of explosions and artillery booms for her radio station, I go to meet a member of my family I never knew existed, who is living on the Lebanese border.

So I am introduced to my 'new' 76-year-old cousin. He has our family tree to hand courtesy of a fantastic computer program he has mastered.

Our history began in Epfig in 1719 when a certain Baruch Elias was born, I discover.

Where the hell is Epfig? I google it. *Epfig is in Alsace, near Strasbourg and Colmar. There is still a beautiful synagogue there; it was built in 1826 and is now a farm, since the Jews disappeared in World War II.* Google is accurate but cold.

The descendants of Baruch – my newly discovered ancestor who grew up when Louis XV was king and Daniel Defoe was writing *Robinsoe Crusoe* – lived in the Alsace and Lorraine for 250 years. They married into families called Levy, Bloch, Kahn and Willard. Some fled to Paris when the Germans took Alsace in the war of 1870.

I am utterly fascinated. I examine our family tree and stop at the marriage of Pierre Willard to Anne Bloch in the 19th century. The couple had a daughter, Sarah Willard, who was my great-grandmother and a son, Isidor Willard, who is Nathan's great-grandfather. We really are cousins.

When Nathan left for Israel in 1950, he was still called Francis Levy. He met his wife Fanny at the kibbutz. Both their parents had been deported and killed by the Nazis. Both he and Fanny were hidden during the 1945 war. When he was fourteen years old, Francis, who came from a middle class professional family in Nancy, was sent to live with peasants. He worked on the farm and in the fields.

Nathan's father was a gynaecologist. His family had been in France for centuries. They did not imagine they could be arrested and deported from their homeland. But his papers marked him as a Jew. The Germans captured him, tortured him because he had treated resistance fighters, and sent him to Drancy, the French concentration camp. He was then deported East in a convoy which finished in Kaunas in Lithuania. There Dr Levy was killed.

'Life was tough,' Nathan explains, 'when the kibbutz started. My first job was to look after the chickens. Then I became the Secretary of the kibbutz and its book keeper.'

His children have left, but he will not. Nor will his wife, whether or not there are missiles falling all around them.

Nathan is a computer lover and he gives me a copy of the family tree.

I'm still revelling in the excitement of the new, meeting a cousin I didn't know existed and learning about my family history. But Tsvi and my new cousin are worried.

'Are you going to stay the night? As soon as night falls the artillery will start going full pelt,' they tell us.

We decide to leave for Tel Aviv before it gets too dark.

As I will report on the last day of the war, the hill does not offer Hanita complete protection.

July 22

It's Saturday evening in Tel Aviv. The beach is full of young people; cafés, bars and restaurants stretch into the Med. The place is as garish as any sparkling seafront in the world – neon signs flash, lights twinkle. The colour of the Frishman beach, which French expats and tourists prefer, is deep red. The French, though, still have not arrived from Paris in great numbers. Loudspeakers ring the beach, bellowing very unmellow Israeli music.

I give my impressions of the North to my friends from Jerusalem; for them it is all very distant and unreal. We still don't know what is really going on in the land battles on the other side of the border. No journalist has been embedded with the Israeli commandos battling with Hezbollah fighters in the villages.

We know nothing about the fighting but *everything about the dead*. This is the first war in which a country hears, almost instantly, of the death of one of its soldiers. The television stations and the press publish the photographs of each dead man, give his life story, interview parents and friends. The anonymous corpse becomes a son, a brother, a boyfriend, a neighbour, a cousin.

As a result, the papers are very thick this weekend. The printed press is in good shape in this country. We see pictures of Major Benjy Hillman, 27 years old, of Sergeant Rafael Muskal, 21, Sergeant Liran Saadjah, 21, and Sergeant Yonathan Sergey Wolsiuk – all of them part of the elite 'Egoz' or 'Nut Head' unit, the Israeli equivalent of the SAS.

The military communiques are spare. These soldiers *'died in exchanges of fire at in the Lebanese village of Maroun-al-Ras.'*

Translate that into the reality of this war. The two Shiite villages of Bint Jbeil and Maroun-al-Ras, a few kilometres from the Israeli border, are strongholds of Hezbollah and the Islamic Resistance. They should have been captured in 24 hours, according to our supreme military strategists, but instead, they have become death traps for the super-commandos. We need to wait for the soldiers to return from Lebanon to get the true story of the fighting.

My friends wait for me at a big table, their feet dangle in the sea, the kids run on the sand. Ariane has come from Jerusalem to dine with us, and jokes that maybe a missile will hit Tel Aviv. Then her mobile beeps with an incoming text message.

URGENT: *Terrorist alert. Avoid the beach at Tel Aviv.'*

The text is no joke. Ariane works for a Minister in Jerusalem.

We look around, no one moves, the music still brays and blares as helicopters arrive overhead. They hover low and sweep the beach with their searchlights. Police patrols stop and search cars. The tension makes us forget how bad the food is.

I call my friends in the press agency and get ready to run to any scene I might have to report from.

'There's been a warning that a suicide bomber is on the way to the port. Apparently a Palestinian girl,' I'm told.

'Should I go there?'

'Just now there is only a huge traffic jam around the port. Because it's Saturday night. We'll tell you the moment we know anything,' they promise.

'And the beach – is that safe?'

'If the information we have is good, you can carry on eating. But we no longer trust official sources.'

So we keep on eating to the rhythm of the helicopters. It's hard to relax in the midst of a scene from *Apocalypse Now*, as the choppers hover low and the downdraft from their blades whisks through our salads.

Then, the squadron of helicopters heads out to sea. No one has pulled the plug on the ghastly music. But the beach empties. Tel Aviv's party-loving natives are worried now and they abandon sea, sand and music. Usually these good life gluttons start eating at midnight and party on till 6 a.m., when they take an invigorating run on the sand. But tonight Hezbollah has destroyed the party spirit.

I call my mates at the news agency which never sleeps, never closes.

'The alert is over. The police have stopped the car with these guys and a Palestinian girl who had come from the territories to make a suicide attempt. It is not totally clear whether or not they were carrying any explosives. Apart from that remember that your Minister is landing,' they say helpfully.

'What Minister?' says the ace reporter, on top of her brief.

'The French Minister for Foreign Affairs, Douste-Blazy. He has taken the shuttle from Beirut to bring peace to the Middle East, of course – and he's brought a party of journalists with him.'

Early the next day, I ask Paris how much of this they want, though I know what they'll say all too well.

'Should I follow Douste during his big day in Israel. Are you interested?'

'Not really.' Editorial is being its usual enthusiastic self.

'Thought so,' I say.

Nevertheless, I decide to follow our Foreign Minister as he strives to bring peace to the region. This is either very brave or very stupid. As I have not applied for accreditation to his press pack, I have not been reserved a place in any official vehicle. Somehow I will have to gate crash the high security that protects our official envoy.

July 23

I start my hunt for Douste at sunrise.

And miss him.

The French Embassy tells me he left for Haifa at dawn, but this doesn't really matter, as the press mini-bus is full. They hand me a deeply newsworthy statement which states that Douste Blazy has come 'to show his solidarity with the victims on both sides'.

Blazing Dust, as I am tempted to call him, is a doctor and was Mayor of Lourdes from 1989 to 2000. Lourdes is the small town in south-west France where a peasant girl called Bernadette Soubirou saw an apparition of the Virgin Mary seventeen times in 1859. As a result, the town is famous for its miracle cures. Maybe he thinks he can perform a miracle.

Douste's first mission is to go to Haifa and leave a wreath at the bombed railway station. There, he gets the treatment we have all come to expect. A siren warns of an incoming Katyusha.

This would be a big hit for Hezbollah, knocking out the French Foreign Minister with one of Stalin's Organs.

The moment they hear the siren, Douste's security men take the minister out of his car and push him into the stairwell of the nearest building.

They are only doing their job. It is sensible to take these warnings seriously; the ball bearing-laden rockets have killed two people today. Across the border in Tyre, Israeli fire kills one press photographer and many families who were not able to flee north.

After four days of fighting, elite Israeli commandos finally capture the village of Maroun-al-Ras one kilometer inside

Summer Rain

Lebanon: Hezbollah admits losing the village but does not say how many of its men have died.

After Blazing Dust emerges from the stairwell, we hear he did not get too stressed. He gets back in his car to keep his appointment in Jerusalem with Tzipi Livni, the Israeli Foreign Minister. I decide to wait for him, hoping I'll get inside the building somehow.

I don't even get into the parking lot. I am not wearing the right badge so a burly security man will not let me pass. The summit meeting and the press conference will have to take place without me.

I am about to abandon my plan of covering the visit of Blazing Dust – which will please my bosses in Paris – when the parking lot barrier is lifted to let the official convoy of cars through with its motorcycle outriders and police escorts. There is no room for me.

Suddenly one car stops. The door opens. A hand is stretched out towards me. It is the James Bond moment.

'Get in and be quick about it,' says the woman press attaché from the French embassy. She feels sorry for me, I think, sweating in the Ministry parking lot. It is a sweltering 35 degrees (my colleagues in Paris would be pleased: 'We told you! Forget about Douste!')

'Thanks,' I say as I grab her hand and get into the car.

I suspect my colleagues in Paris will be less than thrilled by the fact that I have managed to embed myself in the official French party.

I recover from the surprise and ask in a suitably professional tone: 'So what did they say at the press conference?'

'Not much,' a tired voice informs me from the back seat. It belongs to a journalist who has been embedded with Blazing Dust throughout his groundbreaking, *How to Bring Peace in Three Days* trip. So I don't have to worry I've missed something new.

This will be another useless experience, I say to myself.

88

July 23

The situation improves at the French consulate in Jerusalem, where the Minister has to change cars before going on to Ramallah to meet the President of the Palestinian Authority.

I say 'hello' to Douste who, when he was Minister of Culture as well as Mayor of Lourdes and the Grotto, boasted to me of his town's rare charms. I also know him from Toulon, where he backed artists opposing the National Front led by Jean-Marie Le Pen, who has led the extreme right in France since the time of the dinosaurs.

'I missed the press conference with Tzipi Livni,' I say, 'so could I maybe catch up in the car on the way to Ramallah?'

'Okay, get in the back,' Douste says. 'Monsieur le Consul will not mind giving up his place next to me to you.'

So, very 'diplomatically', the Consul (who does mind) is kicked out of the car. I take my seat in the back of the ministerial limo next to Douste. I pounce on the two pathetic sandwiches, which are the only food provided for this groundbreaking, peacemaking minister.

Douste gives me a scoop but nobody, not even myself, realises it at the time.

'The Israelis are ready to accept an international peacekeeping force,' he declares as he takes two bites of the last sandwich.

That morning, Tzipi Livni finally met with her Prime Minister and persuaded him to agree to her diplomatic plan – the one he had rejected a week earlier. But that was kept secret at the time.

So on Sunday July 23, Ehud Olmert finally relaxes his position from his earlier 'we hit them till they crumble' absolutism. He accepts the idea of an international force that will neutralize Hezbollah in southern Lebanon and stop it replenishing its arsenal of weapons. Olmert will no longer insist on the total disarmament of Hezbollah.

That will be the basis of the eventual UN Resolution. Douste has come to Jerusalem at the right time. He also asks Tzipi Livni to stop bombing Beirut Airport so that one of the runaways can be opened to allow humanitarian aid in. She agrees to that.

He has had more luck with her than with Nabih Berri in Beirut. Berri, the president of Lebanon, is close to Hezbollah. Douste asks him to get Hezbollah to release the two Israeli soldiers in exchange for three Lebanese soldiers. Berri does nothing about Douste's request.

Douste also tries to get Jerusalem to agree to release the Palestinian Ministers and MPs who have been in jail since the conflict began. He has no luck there, nor with his proposal for an immediate ceasefire.

But he sees everyone, hoping to convince them, with his boy scout's enthusiasm, of the need to stop the fighting. He is more at ease doing humanitarian deals than with the Byzantine diplomatic negotiations the Quai d'Orsay and the Elysée love so much. Good for him. Boy scouts can get some good results.

We drive out of Jerusalem and reach the checkpoint for entry into Palestinian territory. It is easy to imagine that we are twenty years back at Berlin's Checkpoint Charlie, the only gap in The Wall built to keep East and West Berlin apart. But this Wall here is still standing. It's as if we are in Outer Space. Our convoy goes into a sealed area and then the doors slam shut behind us. We are in no man's land, surrounded by Israeli and Palestinian soldiers, all of them armed to the teeth.

The Minister and I get out of the French limo and into an even more impressive vehicle; the French and Palestinian flags flutter from its sides.

'WELCOME TO PALESTINE!' says the chief of Protocol for the Palestinian President, Mahmoud Abbas. His French is perfect; God bless the Alliance Française, the French cultural institute.

It's quite a moving moment. Suddenly I feel that the State of Palestine really exists and once this seems possible, you start to dream of peace, of two States with a normal border, of two peoples living side by side, of democracy and even of two flourishing economies. The 21st century version of every man (and woman) shall have his or her vine and Levant-issue fig tree.

As we drive into Ramallah, a veritable Armada of vehicles and guards precedes our convoy. The Palestinian Presidential Guard is putting on a fine show as we make our way through the future capital of the future state to the Muqata, the famous headquarters of the late Yasser Arafat. The Muqata is the HQ of the Palestinian Authority.

Around the corner, I see a massive shadow and realise that it is the shadow of the Wall.

The Wall, some 6 metres high, has been built to separate the Palestinians from the Israelis and protect Israel from suicide bombers. The terminology matters to some people – is it a *wall*, or a more innocuous *fence*? The fact is that this wall has made the whole of Palestine into a ghetto. When any Palestinian wants to leave the occupied territories, he or she has to deal with the Wall. The Wall also marks the provisional boundary – of course it will be reviewed but it is a beginning – of the future state of Palestine.

At the entrance to the Muqata, Abbas greets Douste with elegance and dignity. The Palestinian middle class excel at such ceremonies. Greetings over, the two men go to talk with their many advisers and translators – far away from journalists.

During their meeting, I will learn, Douste asks Abbas to free Gilad Shalit. Abbas is only too willing to do it, but he has no control over the people who are holding Shalit and it is almost certain he has no idea where the corporal is actually being held. Shalit is in the hands of Hamas, Abbas' bitter enemy.

The world's press waits while these men of limited power talk. Then we notice a patrol of policemen, or they may be presidential guards, marching past with slow mournful steps. They stop at a discreet mausoleum in the corner of the compound. Then they present arms. We realise they are paying their respects at the tomb of Yasser Arafat.

Thirty minutes later, Abbas and Douste emerge to tell us of a classic diplomatic fudge – or perhaps I should say 'falafel', as we are in the Middle East. In front of the cameras and the mikes, France promises to help the Palestinians, who are being strangled by the Israeli economic blockade imposed since Gilad Shalit was kidnapped. In return, Abbas promises to free the Israeli soldier, though we are all aware that he has no idea where in Gaza Shalit is being held.

'He's very nice and full of good will, Abbas,' says Alex, who rings me from his press agency to get my take on the latest French diplomacy in the Middle East. 'But Abbas has no power. His efforts are meaningless.'

What follows proves Alex is correct. Corporal Shalit is not released by Hamas and the Israeli blockade keeps Gaza cut off from the rest of the world.

Our imposing diplomatic convoy then leaves Ramallah, zig zagging through its narrow streets, like in the movie *Men in Black*, as if someone were chasing us. Then, just as suddenly, we stop. We turn around. There has obviously been a change of plan. We get out of the cars and are surrounded by armed men. We have not been taken hostage: but we are being taken to a restaurant. Excellent, as I'm starving. The great and good of Ramallah are expecting us or, rather, expecting Blazing Dust. The dishes we are offered are much nicer than the sandwiches provided by the French Foreign Ministry.

But we don't have time to eat anything. First there are the elaborate speeches of welcome. It would be very bad manners to stuff myself with food while the diplomatic salaamaleks are being uttered. Then, Douste says that he is very sorry but he has a number of key meetings and he is already late. Falafel-less, humus-less, kebab-less, we get back in the cars.

We return to Checkpoint Charlie. *Goodbye Palestine, Hello Israel.*

Douste is late, but hopes to have time to meet the German Minister of Foreign Affairs who is hanging around the King David Hotel in Jerusalem waiting for him. Memo to French diplomats; do you realise you have a bad reputation when it comes to being on time?

The King David hotel is a historic place. It was blown up by Zionist terrorists in 1946. 28 members of the British security forces were killed along with 17 Jews and 41 Arabs. The Haganah, Israel's own guerillas, argued that the British were preventing refugees from Europe landing, and so the bombing was justified.

At the King David, Douste spends a long time with the mother and father of Corporal Shalit to give them moral support, and explain how he is trying to negotiate the release of their son. Later on, he will meet Olmert, who confirms that he has now abandoned his opposition to a multinational force. The Prime Minister tells Douste that a new version of Finul, the United Nations Peacekeeping Force, might be useful. This is not the triumphant tone Olmert expected he would take when Lord of the Skies Halutz told him the planes had won the war in the first 30 minutes, making the Six Days War seem very slow. But in 1967, there was no question who won and who lost.

'He is not ridiculous, our Minister of Foreign Affairs' I tell my boss in Paris, as I ask for a number of pages to tell the story – *My day with Douste*. Progress is slow but things are moving on the diplomatic front.

'They've fried your brains and you're suffering from *Stockholm syndrome*,' says my less than impressed boss.

Stockholm syndrome, named after a Swedish bank siege, is the psychological process that makes hostages identify with their hijackers; they begin to sympathise with those who hold them prisoner, even coming to feel affection for them.

Inevitably, while the diplomats fudge, the deaths continue.

Summer Rain

The war produced much 'exciting' graphic work – and perhaps this is as good a 'live action' fighting map of the confusion as any.

July 24

I finally meet someone who speaks of 'asymmetrical' war. Napoleon, Wellington, Rommel, Patton, Churchill and Montgomery never knew it, but they had the luck to fight symmetrical wars.

But the rules have changed, and with them the nature of military victory.

The theory of asymmetrical warfare is now used to explain why large armies have no chance of winning an old style 'victory'. They bring out their planes, tanks, and 21st century targeting systems, but the cunning enemy is not playing that game. The guerillas don't come out in a nice red line but break all previous decencies of war and 'embed' themselves among the population. Conventional armies are even more likely to fail against guerillas who are ready to die for their God and their cause.

This war is not the Second World War. It is not the 1948 war of independence, nor the Six Days War. The history of the second part of the 20th century is partly the story of how smart and sneaky guerillas triumphed over mighty military machines. Ironically, one of the first guerilla triumphs was the work of the Haganah, who pushed the British out of Palestine.

Other failures of big armies include:

Indochina – lost by the French.

Algeria – lost by the French (again).

Vietnam (formerly Indochina) – lost by the Americans.

Afghanistan – lost by the Russians.

Now the Americans are bogged down in Iraq, NATO is trapped in Afghanistan, and the Israelis cannot demolish Hezbollah.

I go to discuss the notion of asymmetrical war with Danny Yatom, who I like interviewing, because the former head of Mossad is a practical man.

'Here we are, the most modern army in the world, up against a group of very mobile fighters. They're very hard to infiltrate and so we don't get really good information. Their rockets launchers are in the bushes, in their houses,' Yatom explains.

'They have some of the advantages of little guys but they are not little guys at all, as they have hundreds of millions of Syrians and Iranian dollars behind them. That helps.'

Danny Yatom is now a Labour Member of the Knesset. He has been backing the government's position, but he has no illusions.

'There is no hope of finishing off a terrorist organization just by military means. Even if we killed thousands of them, even if we destroyed thousands of their rockets, they would still be capable of doing damage to us. The way to deal with them is to achieve a diplomatic solution which has lots of military pressure behind it.'

Yatom argues that the Israeli military has not been doing too badly, as it happens.

'Every day our army scores some significant success. In the two weeks we have left, we will not be able to eradicate every last bit of Hezbollah's arsenal, but we can inflict enough damage for them to understand that if the battles continue they will get weaker. Two weeks from now, when the negotiations start, their position will be less strong and ours will be stronger.'

I sense Yatom has some idea of when the government will have to bow to demands for a ceasefire.

He adds: 'In any case that is the strategy – score some points, the faster, the better, in the two or three weeks we have left before the Americans impose a ceasefire.'

'What would be anything like a victory?' I ask him.

'If we managed to push Hezbollah back north of the Litani

river, which is thirty kilometres from the border. Their rockets have a range of thirty kilometres. And if we got back our kidnapped soldiers. And if someone would replace Hezbollah as the power in Southern Lebanon. An international force that would help the Lebanese army take control of that area would be good too.'

No international force will find that easy. Hezbollah-land is full of sympathizers and secret arms dumps, which will remain hidden, waiting for the next time they can surprise Israel.

Today the death toll is great – 334 on the Lebanese side and 18 on the Israeli side. The exodus continues on both sides of the border.

My son, who is diving in the Red Sea and stunned by the beauty of the corals, tells me there is not one room left to rent in Eilat. Tens of thousands of people from the north have started to head south. And Eilat is as far south as you can get in Israel. It is the Las Vegas of the Red Sea and faces the dim lights of Saudi Arabia. Hotels cater for sun worshippers and divers. One of the women involved in Britain's Profumo scandal, Mandy Rice Davies, ran a nightclub there. For some northerners the war is an excuse to take a week off by the Red Sea. They don't imagine that these holidays will last forever.

The exodus is no problem for the rich, who can pick and choose among the luxury hotels. But when you go down the socio-economic scale, it is very different. When people can no longer afford the hotels, they have to seek other accomodation. Everyone has to improvise and rely on the help of family or friends. But Israel is good at handling a crisis. Strangers offer help; groups of people form self-help clubs.

If you don't have money, friends or family because you have just arrived in Israel, you are stuck in the north. No bright lights of Eilat for you. This is the situation that a few hundred Ethiopian Jews find themselves in. In his clever book, *Milk and Honey*, written in 1950, George Mikes suggested that Yemenite Jews would become the Jews of brave new Israel. Now it's the

Ethiopians. For seven years they waited in appalling conditions in Addis Ababa to get permission to fly to the Promised Land.

And lo the day came.

And lo the government settled them on the shore of Lake Tiberias, where no one had seen a single rocket since Biblical times. Until the summer of 2006.

Hezbollah uses its longest-range missiles against Tiberias and duly creates panic. People want to leave, and those who can, do.

The Ethiopians have to take refuge in municipal shelters; the heat is stifling; the only distraction is the TV, whose programmes are in Hebrew, which the Ethiopians do not understand. But they have nowhere else to go.

The government is not too worried about the civilian population. It is totally focused on the war, on how to extract itself and protect the country from further rains of rockets. To save money, the government does not declare a state of emergency. So there is no general mobilization.

The Prime Minister studies the military maps and does not seem concerned by what is a first in the history of Israel. One million of its citizens cannot live normally. They can't go to work, they can't open their shops, they can't walk down the street, they can't buy medicines, as all the chemists are closed, and they can't get any cash because the cash dispensers are empty. The children can't play in the parks or gardens, or even just breathe fresh air.

As Danny Yatom says, Hezbollah has suffered considerable losses, but it is hard to escape the conclusion that they have scored a major political success, not just for themselves but also for their Iranian sugar daddy. They have brought a third of the country to a stop.

So the resistible rise of Iran in 2006 is a hot topic today. Selim Nassib, a French writer who lived in Beirut, notes that the Islamic Republic 'no longer fears the Iraqi army nor the American army. It broadcasts its nuclear ambitions and speaks of wiping Israel off the map. Iran uses its influence in Iraq, where nearly half the population is Shiite, and by supporting Hezbollah, it has become the champion of the sacred Palestinian cause.'

Israel is staring political defeat in the face.

In the evening I have dinner with Noemi Schory, my friend who makes documentaries with both Israeli and Palestinian filmmakers. She was the first Israeli woman to preside at the International Forum of Public TV. She travels from conference to film festival. Usually she displays her cynical and knowing humour when she laughs in great bellows about the incompetence of the government in Jerusalem. But not now. This evening she looks desperately upset. It feels like a catastrophe.

'The destruction in Lebanon with so many victims is dreadful,' she says. 'And utterly useless. What's the point of hitting Beirut airport? Everyone knows that the weapons don't come in by plane but by road. Trucks bring them in from Damascus. This war is dangerous for us because it's changing the way we see ourselves. It's the end of arrogance, the end of feeling that we are invincible. And it's changing the way the rest of the world sees us. The image of Israel is being damaged, damaged beyond repair.'

The top of the map shows Hanita, where the author found
a cousin she knew nothing about

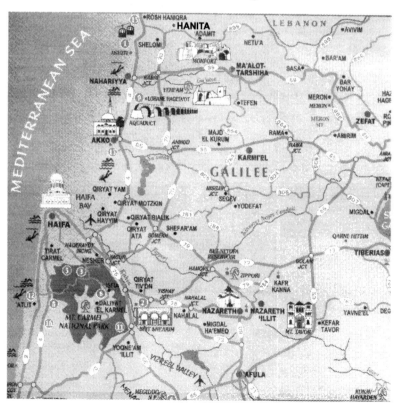

July 25

The government still does not declare a state of emergency. It has failed to destroy Hezbollah. The bombing raids continue and the army sends young – and not so young – soldiers into Lebanon. In the midst of this crisis, Israeli politicians are also beset by scandals about the usual suspects – sex and money. The founders of Israel were socialists, Zionists and idealists. Sixty years later, the country has started to resemble a banana republic.

And remember, a banana is a phallic symbol.

I'll start with the all-too-ready-to-unzip top banana, The President of the State of Israel. Moshe Katsav's job is mainly ceremonial, so he has to open many flower shows, launch ships and cut ribbons like Queen Elizabeth. But he is President of a country at war. Ironically, his very personal problems start the day Hezbollah launches its attacks.

Bad luck, Mr President!

On July 12, 2006, the Attorney General opens a criminal investigation at the request of the President. Katsav claims he has been the victim of a dastardly blackmail plot orchestrated by a ruthless woman. But it seems Katsav is cognitively or neurologically, perhaps, challenged. The police soon discover that the President, who lacks military experience but has been noted for his, as the Spanish say, cojones, does not seem to have his nether anatomy under control.

Katsav comes from Iran. He is married and has five children. He is a member of the right-wing Likud faction and became President after Ezer Weizman resigned suddenly, having been accused of corruption. I told you – Israel is becoming more

101

and more like a real Middle Eastern state.

The police investigation discovers that the 61-year-old President seems to spend many of his office hours propositioning girls. I say 'girls', plural, because it seems this is not a question of one isolated incident. By the time the police wrap up their investigation, five women will have complained that Katsav harassed them sexually. One of them launches a fierce attack on him, appearing on television with her face blurred. She denies that she demanded either money or a better job in return for sexual favours. The truth is the very opposite, she claims. Katsav threatened to dismiss her if she did not have sex with him.

Clinton famously played about with Monica and cigars but she did not complain of sexual harassment. In fact, the poor girl wanted him to harass her rather more. French Presidents have all had their flings, but these never become political scandals.

There is nothing new in politicians finding time in their busy schedules to squeeze in a quick squeeze. That does not pose problems if the women are willing adults and, especially, if the politicians do not have to focus on more important matters of life and death such as incoming missiles and ongoing Intifadas. Clinton's canoodling never seemed to distract him from his duties as President.

But the Israeli president is no Bill Clinton. Katsav apparently used the power of his office to force his unwanted attentions on a junior employee. In 1988, the Knesset passed a law criminalizing sexual harassment. It classified as rape any extortion of sexual favours under threat of dismissal. This law has rarely been used, but now Katsav risks being arrested and charged under it.

Instead of paying up, persuading his accuser to keep quiet or making her Ambassador to Mongolia on a very high salary, Katsav called the cops. And the cops discover that perhaps it is not the President who is the victim here.

The Katsav Affair breaks as the war begins. The President could – and should – have played a key role as a political and moral sage advising Olmert. Instead, Katsav has to answer questions – let me couch this diplomatically – about who screwed who on the Presidential couch. He does not handle the situation well.

'I am a victim of the press which is carrying out a witch-hunt against me. I am the victim of a lynching where there has been no trial,' Katsav wails, but the press can't help but notice that he does not give very precise details about what did – or did not – happen. He does not handle the situation well.

The army is bogged down in Lebanon; the President of Israel seems to have been caught with his trousers down. It begins to feel like a soap opera.

Katsav is not the only powerful man to become a victim of his physical impulses. One of the most effective spokesmen for the government is Haim Ramon, but he too has succumbed to the disease I shall label *Politician's Prick*. The flamboyant 65-year-old Minister of Justice appears to have forced a kiss on a 21-year-old woman working for the army.

When and where? The 'why' seems obvious enough. The kiss took place at 19.45 in the office of the Prime Minister, a few minutes before the key Cabinet meeting: the main item on the agenda was how to respond to Hezbollah, and whether to declare war.

The young officer had just finished her military service and was about to be photographed with a number of ministers when Ramon was provoked beyond endurance by her rosy red lips.

The government of men with no military experience and inflated cojones now gets into a total macho stew. It would be insane to deprive the government of the brilliant services of Ramon at a time of national emergency because he snatched a kiss. This is feminism run amok. A kiss is not so serious.

Balls and Neanderthal balls, is the gist of the reply provided by Galia Golan Gilad, professor of political science and a specialist in the rights of women. 'To stick your tongue down the unwilling throat of an unwilling woman is a crime. That is not some loony feminist gripe but the law of the land.'

Hamon will resign and be found guilty of indecent assault.

It's shekels as well as sex. The press now learns that the Chief of Staff, Dan 'Wings' Halutz, took time off on July 12 to ring his stockbroker and sell off his portfolio of shares. Halutz's portfolio is worth only $20,000 or $30,000 so it's small beer compared to the investments of Israeli tycoons, but the timing is as bad as it can get. Halutz sells his stocks after Hezbollah have attacked, but before the military operation starts that evening. Hardly the act of a confident leader. The God of Stock Markets punishes Wings, as the Tel Aviv Exchange does not crash but stays quite stable. Investors have faith in the government and the mighty military.

Then we come to the Prime Minister himself. Ehud Olmert's past as Mayor of Jerusalem is catching up with him. When he ruled the Holy City, it seems he handed out building permits to a few friends who happened to be major property developers. As you do. There is absolutely no connection between the not-really-favours he did for the developers and the big discount they gave him when he bought a new flat – a nice little reduction of $500,000. An inquiry has also been launched into Olmert's role in the sale of one of Israel's top banks, the Bank Leumi.

When he was Mayor of Jerusalem, Olmert did not have a good reputation when it came to money. Nevertheless, having met him a few times, I have to accept that he has some qualities. He was a right-wing hawk, yet managed to persuade Ariel Sharon to expel the Jewish settlers and hand Gaza back to the Palestinians. It was historic, brave, necessary and a good move towards a peaceful solution. Sadly, the Palestinians did not respond in kind but continued to lob their Qassams into the Negev.

'Will all the mistakes it has made in the war bring down the government?' I ask Alex, who understands the Israeli political class well.

'No, you'll see, if Olmert has to resign it won't be because of the war but because of his property deals and other allegations of corruption. Our politicians are corrupt – like everywhere – but the legal system works, the judges are not bent and the press does its work well.'

Alex will turn out to be right. Olmert will survive the mistakes of the war.

I ought to mention here a fact of Israeli politics. Every year the papers ask people to vote on 'the most corrupt politician of the year'. Britain prides itself on the tabloid press and its heavyweight political critics but do *Channel 4* or *The Spectator* have an award for the most corrupt politician of the year? No. Israel was set up to be a beacon unto the nations and is pioneering an almost official award for political corruption.

In November 2006, Olmert will win this coveted prize. He gets nearly 50% of the votes while Amir Peretz, the Minister of Defence, comes third. Tzipi Livni, the Foreign Minister, is the least corrupt 'man' in the government, followed by Shimon Peres.

Then comes the first big shift in policy. On July 25, Olmert accepts that an international United Nations Force should help keep the peace in southern Lebanon. It is a big success for the diplomats.

But then, at 19.25, a missile carrying 500 kilos of explosives smashes into the United Nations post at Khiam. It was fired from an Israeli air plane. Four unarmed UN observers are killed – one Canadian, one Austrian, one Chinese, and one Finn.

This 'accident' will truly encourage countries to send their men to take part in keeping the peace and neutralizing Hezbollah. Olmert apologises in the name of Israel. *'This was an accident which the government deeply regrets.'*

But Kofi Annan, the Secretary General of the United Nations, is livid and not to be mollified. He hints that the attack was deliberate, and so Israel now has the world's No. 1 diplomat undiplomatically angry. Some suspect that the real reason the missile was launched at Khiam is that the military have been furious for years at United Nations 'peacekeepers' who did nothing to prevent Hezbollah building up its arsenal and digging its secret tunnels.

If only, we will discover in one of the many inquiries after the war. The real reason is staggeringly pathetic.

'Our maps were out of date,' the military eventually explain. The army was using maps that dated from 2000, and the United Nations Post at Khiam was not marked on them. No wonder the secret services can't infiltrate Hezbollah.

As the war progresses, it becomes clear that all the high-tech gadgets are not as useful as the old human trick of infiltrating the enemy. But Hezbollah is hard to infiltrate. The terrorists aren't just linked by their beliefs, they come from the same villages and belong to the same families. They know each other's brothers, cousins, and sisters. Strangers stand out.

The facts will get more embarrassing, as I hinted earlier, writing about July 12. After the war, army officers reveal they screamed, begged and implored to obtain all the information the secret files contained on bunkers and Hezbollah. But the Intelligence Directorate did not hand over these secret files because they were too 'secret'.

There is an Israeli joke. A man runs out of the Mossad building and leaps into a taxi.

'Where are you going?' the driver asks.

'I couldn't possibly tell you,' the Mossad man replies.

Finally, the army received the sealed boxes of secret files from Intelligence after a week of war, a week of fighting without intelligence against the Hezbollah militia, which led to their bombing the wrong targets.

The media are suffering too. Shlomo Papirblat is tired. By

the 13th day of the war, the editor of the largest circulation daily paper in Israel is beginning to feel the pressure. Every day *Yedioth Ahronot* publishes pictures of the soldiers who have died in combat and of the civilians who have been killed by the missiles. The toll is now 50 dead, 35 of whom were soldiers. On the Lebanese side, 405 people have died, including 339 civilians. But it is hard to be exact, as Hezbollah does not report its dead.

Shlomo is the author of a bestselling book on wine and we share an excellent glass of red in the old harbour of Tel Aviv. We watch the sea and talk but he has to keep an eye on the clock, as he must return to the office to put his paper to bed.

When the war started Shlomo was enthusiastic and backed the government. But 13 days on, he is anxious and full of questions.

'Our country is crap but it's the only one we have,' he tells me. 'Our forces aren't doing too well but we don't happen to have another army.' He is adapting the words of a song that has become something of a hit in the last two weeks.

These sayings become slogans for the young who have been brought up here, in a country that has been at war for most of its life. They did not choose to live here, but they have nowhere else to go. Why else do they write: *'I have no other country'* on their T-shirts?

July 26

This morning David Grossman, the author of *Yellow Wind*, publishes another remarkable text. Grossman is both a magnificent novelist and a peace activist, who started out by supporting the government's action against Hezbollah. It was legitimate, he said, but now Grossman voices a really unwelcome truth – the army is no longer invincible and its deterrent capacity has been compromised.

'For all these years Tsahal has been used to confront the Palestinians and the settlers. The occupation of the territories and its complication, the occupation and its insanity, have taken up all our energies for years.'

Grossman argues that the army has been turned into a repressive and oppressive police force, which has lost its edge, because it has been controlling Gaza and the West Bank and that has been almost too easy. He seizes the moment to argue that: *'... we must talk with the Palestinians. They have every interest in making peace with Israel.'* He adds: *'Hezbollah intends to destroy Israel but the most of the Palestinians have accepted – maybe reluctantly – the existence of Israel and the need to divide the land we share. A wise idea would be for Israel to start negotiations with the Palestinians even before the combat with Hezbollah ends. That would show the Palestinians and, indeed, the rest of the world that Israel can tell the difference between these fronts – and could improve its position.'*

It seems wise. But Grossman is under no illusions. The radio tells us that today Israeli raids in Gaza killed 27 Palestinians – ten of them were activists from militant factions, but two were little girls. One was three years old, the other only seven months. Hardly terrorists!

Have these raids helped free Corporal Shalit? Have they stopped the rockets raining down on Israel? Have they succeeded in destroying Hamas by killing its chiefs?

While the battle of Lebanon has been raging, the war against Palestine has continued. 153 Palestinians have been killed since July 12.

The government does not take heed of Grossman's suggestions but continues to fight on two fronts; it also bombs Gaza, targeting the leaders of Hamas though not quite with unerring accuracy. Anyone who happens to be physically close to a Hamas leader in a busy street, or in a house, may get killed too. 'Collateral damage' is inevitable, we're told.

At this point we see a manifestation of Israeli political genius. Jerusalem finds it politically appropriate to seize and imprison most of the Palestinians ministers. These men were democratically elected, and there were fewer quibbles about the elections in Gaza than in Florida when Bush 'beat' Gore. Beacon Israel is supposed to support democracy and teach its benefits to the less 'advanced' Arabs. The brilliant idea is that if 'we' seize more of their leaders, we will be in better position to bargain for 'our' kidnapped soldier.

But now it's thug against thug here in the Holy Land. The clever tactic does not seem to work. Young Corporal Shalit stays in the hands of his captors.

My next meeting is with a man who won the Nobel Peace Prize but on my way to see him, I stumble in a hole on the pavement. I was looking up as I walked, admiring the magnificent architecture of the world capital of the Bauhaus movement. Tel Aviv's superb buildings have aged since the 1930s, but they are starting to be restored, rather than being demolished by developers who think the best buildings in the world have big aluminium windows overlooking the sea. I am gazing in admiration at these Bauhaus balconies, when my heel snags on the pavement; ace reporter stumbles, lands on her face and twists her ankle.

July 26

I can't walk at all.

But I do not want to cancel my interview with Shimon Peres as Editorial is really excited by the prospect. The French love him, but the Israelis joke that 'Shimon couldn't win an election in his own family'.

As leader of the Labour Party, Peres lost general elections in 1977, 1981, 1988, and 1996. His one pyrrhic victory, in 1984, saw Labour win more seats than any other faction – but still too few to form a left-wing coalition. He was forced to co-habit with the right-wing Likud, alternating as Prime Minister with Yitzhak Shamir, to whom Peres then lost the next election. He was later defeated in a close race by Binyamin Netanyahu. Peres then lost contests for the Presidency and Labour leadership. His refusal to ever be bowed by defeat has allowed this historic loser to wield astonishing influence. Perhaps more than any other living politician, he embodies Churchill's dictum to 'never, ever, ever give up'.

He became Deputy Prime Minister when he lead the Labour Party into Ariel Sharon's coalition, later defecting to Sharon's breakaway Kadima faction when he lost the leadership to Amir Peretz. In June 2007, Peres was finally rewarded for his perseverance and elected President.

Finally, I find a taxi and make it to Peres' office.

The co-signatory of the famous Oslo Accords, along with Yitzhak Rabin and Yasser Arafat, Peres is a charming man. He is not bothered by waging war on two fronts.

'Today we have a quartet of terror,' Peres tells me. 'On the one hand two states, Syria and Iran. A state trying to establish itself, Hamas, and then a state within another state, Hezbollah.'

Yesterday he spoke at the Knesset. 'It's Hezbollah or us!' He spoke stridently, like a leader rallying his troops. As he is 84, he is unlikely to be called up as a reservist.

'What is the point of bombing Lebanon?' I ask.

'We are not bombing Lebanon, we are bombing Hezbollah,' Peres replies. He makes good eye contact and his voice does

111

not waver. He is not being totally truthful though. Hezbollah is not hiding out on the runway of Beirut Airport. 'If Lebanon and the international community want us to stop bombing the airport, they have to stop Hezbollah.'

He adds that I really should try to understand what is happening on the ground and explains the A to Z of the conflict to a military innocent.

'Our army is destroying the strongholds and fortifications of Hezbollah and its rocket launchers,' he tells me.

Peres may sound bellicose now, but he was the only member of the government to express any doubts on July 12, when the decision was taken to bomb Lebanon.

'Okay, we send in the bombers, but what do we do *after* that?' he asked.

Peres doesn't know that, as he speaks, there is a big problem with the attempt to destroy Hezbollah's fortifications.

For 48 hours, Israeli troops have been attacking Bint Jbeil, which will become the site of the most important battle of this war. Here, a mere three miles across the border, the Israelis have not managed to destroy Hezbollah's positions. They have not even managed to dislodge the Shiite militia. Israeli tanks and soldiers are themselves surrounded. They lose eight men and many more are injured.

No one knows Hezbollah's casualty figures, but we do know the fighting is intense and the Party of God is losing many men.

Day and night the battle rages.

I get back to the apartment in Tel Aviv, limping. Another small example of collateral damage.

My son has got back from the Red Sea and its corals. He looks at the bed which has been made ready for him by the window.

'It faces north,' he says.

'Yes.'

'Well never mind,' he says and falls asleep very quickly. My teenage son is a fatalist.

July 27

The night has been calm. Nothing disturbed the north face of our building. My son slept peacefully. Neither Hezbollah nor Al Qaeda (which has smarmed its way into the action, at least verbally, and says it is all for the destruction of Israel), nor Iran, have decided to launch a missile at Tel Aviv. Yet.

But when I wake up, the news is bad. Yesterday was a national tragedy.

The papers have pictures of nine dead soldiers; not eight, as was believed last night. Three of them are officers; all the casualties are from the elite Golani unit; they were killed by Hezbollah fighters at the never-ending battle of Bint Jbeil. This war is a long way from finished, let alone won.

Israel is not used to military reverses. The last one came during the Yom Kippur war of 1973, and it did not last long. Within a week US Secretary of State Henry Kissinger had to stop Ariel Sharon from capturing the Pyramids, just outside Cairo. Now the stark change of tone in the press signals a growing crisis of confidence. Writers ask; 'Why send commandos to get themselves massacred? Why have we not sent our tanks across the border? How is the militia of the Party of God managing to inflict damage on the best army in the world? What is our military strategy?'

The reply of Chief of Staff Halutz is enormously strategic, not to mention reassuring. 'From a strategic point we have inflicted great damage on Hezbollah,' he says.

And if that's the case, we shouldn't be too bothered about any tactical reverses. Hezbollah launches more and more rockets, holds out against 'our' elite commandos and is not cowed into submission by 'our' bombs. But we're winning the strategic battle. The big picture is good.

Disastrous tactics, fantastic strategies, these must be the ingenious definition of success in modern warfare. Everyone starts to realise that this is not going to be quick and easy. South Lebanon is not Gaza.

The army finally decides to see what manpower it has in reserve. It calls up 18,000 of the nearly 500,000 reservists – three divisions. Men of all ages, who were quietly getting on with their everyday lives, are called up to fight alongside young conscripts.

Haim, the waiter with long hair who works at the restaurant on the beach, is typical. He is not gung-ho about going to war, but he is ready.

'I've got my bag with my things in the car,' he explains as he brings us humus and beer. 'As soon as I get the word on my mobile, I have to join my unit at our secret rendezvous.'

'You're going to the army with your pony tail?'

'I'm a reservist, they don't give a damn about my hair,' he says.

July 28

Unlike Haim, Marcus Sheff does not sport long hair or Rastafarian weaves. He works in communications and speaks good English. He is unlikely to be asked to join the Moroccan and Ethiopian commandos attacking Bint Jbeil.

He works at Army HQ in Haifa, where is it his job to look after the international press. He doesn't just look British, he has a British sense of humour, though he does not often show it. Most of the time he speaks woodenly, giving nothing away. He often resorts to a perfectly pleasant *no comment*.

I was with him in Haifa when the missiles fell like firecrackers and reporters ran in every direction, but Marcus was the image of calm in a crisis. That is a very British trait. In his *How to Be an Alien*, George Mikes described a scene during the Second World War, when he was drinking in a country pub with a Colonel. The alarm sounded, warning of an incoming V–2 rocket. Far from acting calm, the very British Colonel dived for cover under the bar. When no bomb fell and the all clear sounded, he got to his feet and said to Mikes.

'Were you so scared you couldn't move, old chap?'

Mikes was flabbergasted by his chutzpah, as the British don't call it.

The reporters in Haifa don't have such cool when the missiles hit.

Later Marcus put away his uniform and went back to his life as a Tel Aviv yuppie. He also wrote a piece, *The Reservist and the International Press*, for the website of Papirblat's paper, *Yedioth Ahanarot*.

Marcus was angry. He said:

'Last Sunday a Hezbollah attack killed Shimon Glickblich, a sixty-year-old social worker who was driving in Haifa. He had gone to see someone when the siren sounded a second time. At that very precise moment I was with an American journalist. We flung ourselves in a ditch and he started a discussion with me on our chances of survival.

'I believe profoundly we have the same chance of being killed by a missile whether we are driving at 60 mph or standing still on a sidewalk, I say to him. He disagrees. But this is also the day Habib Ouad is killed in his carpenter's workshop in north Haifa, and the poor man was certainly not doing carpentry at 60 mph.'

Marcus adds:

'I am interviewed for a European radio station. The interviewer looks at me askance when I say that Haifa has a mixed Arab and Jewish population and that, as we speak, both are sitting in the shelters trying to keep themselves safe from Hezbollah's rockets. I am surprised he finds that information so irritating. I dare not tell him that earlier today, an Arab man pointed out his shop which had been bombed and said to me that he hoped the army would dispose of Hezbollah.'

It's true enough. Like Marcus, I have talked to many Israeli Arabs who are standing shoulder to shoulder with the Jews in their town. The two peoples of Haifa are still united.

But this historic alliance is under pressure. Israeli Arabs in Acre, in Nazareth, in the villages of northern Galilee, are starting to mutter that they are glad to see the mighty Israeli army is being given a bloody nose by Hezbollah. They don't shout that with joy, but many of them feel a certain satisfaction.

'The solidarity of the citizens of Israel is an illusion,' says Hassan Ali who speaks for the Arab town of Majdal Krum.

Israeli Arabs are not waving Hezbollah flags, but they watch the Arab TV stations, Al Jazeera and Al Manar, and they identify with the victims of Israeli raids on Lebanon – a few miles from their houses.

The Palestinians of Gaza and Nablus do not mutter quietly,

however. Every report of a rocket that kills Jews is greeted with loud hurrahs of praise for their new hero, Hassan Nasrallah.

This Friday, unfortunately, Marcus is not in Haifa. The press circus seems to have shifted its attention north of the border. The TV stations are bored with Israel and prefer to focus on more dramatic images of dead and wounded in Lebanon, and the wretched ruined landscapes of bombed villages. Sounds of artillery fire have become so common they don't even merit 10 seconds in the news bulletins.

I drive back to Tel Aviv. The city seems calm at first, and, then, suddenly, everyone starts to panic. The mobile phones go crazy. The town of Afula, which is only 30 minutes drive away, has been hit by a missile, though it lands harmlessly in a field. Rumour has it that Hezbollah is gunning for the seaside resorts of Herzilya and Natanya, close to Tel Aviv. Will Hezbollah manage to hit Tel Aviv? That's what obsesses people now. And it's not surprising.

From Lebanon, 'badly damaged' Hezbollah has managed to blast a Fajr 5 missile far, far indeed, into the heart of Israel.

For non-specialist readers, the Farj 5 is an Iranian missile which can carry 150 kilos of explosive and has a range of 75 kilometres.

Did Hezbollah miss Tel Aviv because they are just not good enough or is this some subtle political ploy by the wily Nasrallah? Or are they afraid of unleashing unspeakable revenge if they hit the town? No one can ask the Iranians who handed these missiles to their allies, so we can't answer any of these questions.

On the face of it, Tel Aviv shrugs off the threat, but some people leave to sleep in Jerusalem. The city is holy, but, more to the point, it has the great merit of being beyond the range of all Hezbollah's rockets.

July 29

My ankle still hurts from when I tripped over. I put my pink sandals on again – the only ones I can bear – and head north, this time without Jil, who has flown back to Paris. She is on the phone at all hours so that I can update her, reporting exactly what is going on as if we were still driving together.

At Army HQ, Marcus the Brit has been replaced by an older officer who wears a skullcap on his head and carries a machine gun. This man seems to speak every language on earth perfectly.

It is Shabbat.

'For a religious Jew like you,' I ask, 'isn't it a problem having to make phone calls and drive?' I don't add, 'Not to mention carrying your machine gun?'

'It's war,' he says, as he lights a cigarette, which is forbidden on the Sabbath.

His phone buzzes in his ear. He signals something important is being said.

'Follow me, we have to go off at once,' he then says softly.

I don't argue and I limp to my car.

The jeep in front of me starts and takes absolutely no notice of the red light.

I have to follow because I really can't afford to lose it. The jeep speeds towards Lebanon.

Half an hour later, the jeep drives into Acre, which is as empty as Haifa. Every sane person has scurried to the shelters as rockets are raining down on the old Crusader town. The jeeps head for the Beach Hotel which tourists have deserted and the army has requisitioned.

The multi-lingual Major tells me solemnly that I am to get my wish and interview some commandos.

Finally, I will hear what happened at Bint Jbeil.

The battle was so bloody that the army has offered the commandos a bit of relaxation on the beach before it sends them back to the front. The men all belong to the famous Golani unit which was formed in 1948 during the War of Independence. It has a reputation for being hard; its men have always volunteered for especially dangerous missions. The unit now attracts idealistic new immigrants.

A few hours before I meet them, these young men were in southern Lebanon. At dawn they were put on buses and driven here to recover before they go back in. They are shocked. Their unit lost eight comrades at Bint Jbeil when they fell into a trap. Just before that happened, four other men died at Maroun-al-Ras.

'It's a suicidal mission,' one soldier tells me.

'If we go back there we won't come back, we'll die,' another soldier says. Both talk very quietly.

They have taken off their uniforms and are wearing bathing suits, but they keep their machine guns close to their shoulders.

Joseph is 22 years old and has seven men under his command. He looks extremely pale and is very aware of the fact that he has to re-build his men's morale so that they can fight on when they go back to Lebanon. And he knows they have no more than 48 hours 'rest'.

'I'll never forget what happened,' he tells me. He can't hold the glass I offer him; he can't swallow any food. He has not slept for three days.

He speaks of *Platoon*, Oliver Stone's's film about Vietnam.

'It was like in the movie, gunfire everywhere and I saw terrorists falling. I was surprised to see men in neat uniforms with their military badges covered in black cloth so they didn't shine in night. They are a proper army, very motivated. Like we are.'

July 29

The Golani commandos crossed the border at midnight on July 26. In the dark their officers informed them, rather briefly, of their mission: *'You are going to Lebanon to stop the rockets being fired on Israel.'*

They have the best night vision equipment, and believe that the enemy can't see in the dark. But the enemy knows the lie of the land, every shrub and bush, every hiding place.

At 4 a.m., Hezbollah ambushes the unit. Lt Colonel Rooe Klein, who is 31 years old, is marching at the head of the troops. He throws himself on a grenade hurled by Hezbollah to save the men behind him. He is the first Israeli soldier to be killed.

The two Golani units fight their way through and reach the deserted houses of Bint Jbeil, headquarters of the local Islamic resistance. They find bunkers, arms and documents. But they do not find any breakfast – and the army, in its wisdom, has forgotten the first rule of warfare, which was probably old when the Romans decreed that 'an army marches on its stomach'.

'We had nothing to eat,' says Joseph. 'We thought we would be back in twelve hours so we just took a little water with us.'

So breakfast consists of a few raw potatoes they find in the abandoned houses. They lock themselves in, surrounded by the Hezbollah men, and wait.

'We shoot. We shoot, we kill many terrorists but they are immediately replaced by other terrorists.'

The army that does not provide food or water, also does not have a plan for getting the dead and wounded out of this hell hole.

'Four of my comrades are killed,' Joseph says, 'but there are four others who are wounded. I see they are losing blood, but they are in front of the house. We can't go out and rescue them. Their screaming is awful, they're in terrible pain.'

This might be the moment for the helicopters or Halutz's paratroopers to fly to the rescue. But it doesn't happen.

'They die in agony,' Joseph finishes. His hands are trembling.

For three nights and two days, the Golani unit is pinned down at Bint Jbeil. Finally the unit communicates with the Air Force, which manages to drop some useful bombs for once – i.e. they land on Hezbollah, rather than on civilians – and lift the siege so that Joseph's men can come out of the house and pick up their dead and wounded. The commandos then walk two kilometres to a clearing where the helicopters can land and extract the wounded without being hit by Hezbollah missiles.

The dead are not airlifted out. 'Once the choppers left we walked with the dead in body bags, trying not to look at them, in case the body was that of a good friend.'

The soldiers also drag back some bodies of Hezbollah fighters. These will be useful in any exchanges.

But the lads face one last danger – minefields. A team of mining engineers has put white string on the path so that the soldiers can make it back without stepping on the mines, which were laid by Israeli soldiers when they left Lebanon in 2000.

When they reach the border, some men break down crying; others kiss the land of Israel. They all want to know:

'*So have we succeeded in stopping the rockets?*'

Today, Saturday, Hezbollah launched 150 missiles at the north of Israel.

In the article I file, the soldiers speak for the first time of the failures of this war.

But I don't dare publish what some of them confide to me. Some of the soldiers chose to injure themselves so that they would not have to go back to Lebanon. Some fell down stairs deliberately in the hope of breaking a bone.

I don't write that the army is scared of suicides and has dispatched psychiatrists to speak to the soldiers as these are rumours I cannot confirm yet.

I don't write about the parents who arrive at the Beach Hotel and take their weeping sons into their arms. I don't write about the pathetic sweets and ice creams the army provides for its boys, boys who will have to risk their lives one more time.

'We took a beating. So did they. Now we know them,' the soldiers say, as they prepare to go back into battle.

But they know something is amiss in their almighty army. How could their officers have sent them into such a situation without food or logistical support? It's as if the army has not been trained for real war any longer, as David Grossman suggested.

I go on to the beach with the boys during the day. They are all so young – Russians, Ethiopians, Ukrainians, French, and Canadians, who came in the last waves of immigration, or kibbutzniks who have grown up in Israel.

'We came directly from Gaza to fight at Bint Jbeil. We had no preparation and no explanation. We're used to fighting against Hamas in Gaza or the West Bank.' They explain that the 'operations' in the territories are usually targeted killings, blowing up houses, the knock on the door at midnight. There they have to act like tough police who pursue terrorists. Their chiefs did not prepare them to fight professional soldiers who are well-drilled and properly equipped with the latest high-tech materiel.

In an amateur video made by the reservists themselves and later screened on Israeli TV, an officer addresses the exhausted soldiers sitting on the ground. He talks to them about the 'terrorists' they will meet in Lebanon.

'Why do you call them terrorists?' says one of his men. 'They are soldiers like us.'

With remarkable synchronicity, Jean-Pierre Perrin, the special correspondent of *Libération*, manages to get into Bint Jbeil, which the Israelis have now left. Our pieces make it possible to tell the story from both sides.

'The yellow flag of Hezbollah, with its black Kalachnikov, flutters over the ruins of Bint Jbeil. It flutters over a town that no longer exists, a town that could have been caught in an earthquake. Israeli soldiers had to leave the town in the hands of Hezbollah but you don't see a soul – no soldiers and no ordinary men and women. Apart from one old blind woman, who can't walk.'

On his way into town, Jean Pierre meets refugees who are taking advantage of the unofficial truce to flee. They carry a few bags and push the wounded in wheelchairs.

'At the Islamic Hospital of the martyr Salah Gandou – Teheran pays for the hospital and Hezbollah runs it – Dr Fouad kept working during the battle. He treated 160 people in ten days, he says, but he believes the ruined buildings are full of dead bodies. Israeli soldiers got to within 150 metres of the hospital before they were beaten back.'

I take a young Golani in my car. 'I dream of seeing the beach at Tel Aviv,' he says. He has managed to get leave for the night. He's eating the sweets he was given at the Beach Hotel – finally, the therapeutic sugar – and he holds his machine gun. He needs to talk and all the way to Tel Aviv – 90 minutes on the motorway – he speaks, as if he is describing a film *'Two Days and Three Nights in the Hell of Bint Jbeil'*.

'We marched with 40 kilos on our back, stupid and useless equipment and there was nothing to eat, not even campaign rations. We didn't eat for three days so we went crazy with hunger and thirst. The first night I walked by the side of our commanding officer and suddenly we were hit by fire and grenades. The boss jumped to grab a grenade and it exploded. Once we lost him we felt bloody low. Then we lost an Ethiopian guy – there's another one in our unit. The wounded could have survived if the choppers had come for them earlier. We were stuck in those houses in Bint Jbeil without knowing why we were there. We were told to destroy Hezbollah but we saw nothing. I just saw one Hezbollah guy, who was peering in at our windows. I shot at him and woke the others.'

Lebanon 2006 has become a nightmare for the young soldiers, for the reservists and for the army high command. The Lebanese find it just as traumatic.

But in Tel Aviv, people seem less aware because they are relatively far away from the action. It takes 3 to 4 hours to drive to the border. Israelis say Tel Aviv is a Bubble or call it 'Yuppietown'.

The tanned surfers ride the waves, the beach and bars are busy. Tel Aviv's beautiful people drink as the sun sets. The music bellows, a tinny Hebrew euro-pop. Up above, a squadron of F-16s wheels to the north. We hardly notice them.

The soldier and I sit in a fashionable bar. I'm really uneasy bringing him from the trauma of the fighting to this razzle dazzle of the apparently unknowing and unthinking young.

'You don't mind being in the middle of people having fun. You don't resent them?' I ask.

'No I'm fighting so that they can surf, get pissed, have a joint, live a normal life.'

He's not being ironic and I'm impressed. The manager of the bar, who must be over thirty, taps him on the shoulder. He's recognized the laser-guided machine gun that the soldier is still clutching.

'I am also in the Golani,' says the manager. 'I'll probably get called up soon. Take care *brother*.'

This is Tel Aviv style – laconic and relaxed. They are middle class and more likely to have made money in IT than to be working ordinary jobs like the Russians and Ethiopians. The modern and 'we only go to synagogue for weddings and barmitzvahs' Tel Aviv crowd also knows how to avoid serving in combat units.

'I know where I go to attend the burials of soldiers,' says Major General Stern on army radio. 'I go to the kibbutzim, who have had heavy losses, and to funerals of Ethiopian and Russian immigrants, but I hardly ever have to go to Tel Aviv.'

The idealism on which the State was founded is not entirely dead, however. There are signs of it amongst the very patriotic new immigrants and amongst the kibbutzim.

As the war progresses, the good time boys and girls of Tel Aviv are starting to get it in the neck from the press. It is beginning to be noticed that only two residents of Bubbletown have died as a result of the war.

'When are they also going to be hit by an Iranian rocket?' people ask outside the Bubble.

Then *Maariv*, Israel's second largest newspaper, does something that is astonishing in the middle of a war. It runs a ten page investigation on '*Why so many of our readers hope that Nasrallah will actually make good his threat and launch a rocket at Tel Aviv.*'

The answer seems to be that the inhabitants of the Bubble have annoyed the rest of the country. Yuppietown's 'decadents' have continued to swim in the mornings, do business during the day and frolic in the evenings. But the story is not entirely negative. Tel Aviv can be proud, because people there have also put up refugees from the north, looked after their children and organized entertainment for them.

Like the rest of Israel, Tel Aviv has been glued to the radio and television news. And, like the rest of Israel, everyone who lives there is scared the phone will ring and bring terrible news – that a brother, a son, a cousin, or a friend has been killed or wounded.

Many have waited for the phone call that tells them to report to their units. And got it.

Like everyone in Israel, the average inhabitant of Tel Aviv is afraid of the missiles with their lethal cargo of iron shards and ballbearings. But they have not renounced having fun. It is their way of resisting.

July 30

'It's what I was afraid of since it started,' Alex says. 'The government and these military idiots will pursue their bullshit till it can't get any worse.'

In principle Alex supports the right to fuck up and cock up. We hold these principles to be self-evident, as the Declaration of Independence did not quite say – life, liberty, the pursuit of happiness and a few cock-ups here and there. But there are limits – especially in war.

And one limit is 'thou shalt not make the same mistake twice at the same place'.

The military now repeat the cock-up of April 18, 1996 when, previously, it was fighting Hezbollah; the operation had been given another of those poetic names. *The Grapes of Wrath*. I can't help but wonder why the Israeli Army is paying homage to the farmworkers of Steinbeck's masterpiece about the Depression of the 1930s.

In 1996, the ever-accurate military accidentally dropped a shell on the shelter of the United Nations Peacekeeping force at Cana, just south of Tyre. 102 civilians died. The slaughter turned into a victory for Hezbollah, as Israel was forced to negotiate.

Ten years later, in the early hours of the morning, two bombs are dropped on a small building in Cana. Israeli pilots think they are destroying an arsenal of rockets but, in fact, refugees have taken shelter in the building's garage. Many are women and children. The building crumbles, burying the garage. 54 people die in the rubble, including 37 kids. The whole world denounces the second massacre at Cana.

The military explain that there was an arsenal of weapons and missiles next to the building. The pilots released their bombs because the telemetry told them there were rockets below.

'If we had had any idea there were civilians in the buildings, we would not have dropped the bombs,' the military explain. The army apologises to the world, but it can't apologise to the dead.

It doesn't help, of course, that journalists describe the small bodies that are pulled out of the ruins. Hezbollah provides figures, but no one has the stomach to make an inventory of the dead.

Israel has suffered a moral defeat and Hezbollah a media victory but it manipulates the body count and airbrushes the photos to make the carnage look worse than it was. The Party of God does not scruple to take a photo of one dead baby and then insert it into one background after another, so that this poor infant dies many times over to make a propaganda point. Adnan Hajj takes one of these photos. Reuters then sells Hajj's photograph all over the world. The caption runs: *'A rescuer carries the body of a baby who died in the Israeli raid on Cana which killed more than 60 people, most of them women and children.'*

This same rescuer, whose bullet proof-vest peeks out from under his civilian shirt, exhibits the body of the poor baby in a number of places. The man, Salam Daher, is in charge of civil defence in Tyre. He is the person who announces casualty figures to the press. Daher has missed his true vocation, as he excels at producing dramatic and grisly images. The photo of the dead baby travels round the world. Adnan Hajj is later dismissed by Reuters, when bloggers prove that he manipulated the already horrific images with Photoshop to make them look even worse.

The hospital at Tyre is perhaps the only organization to emerge from this tragedy with any credit. Some days later it has the courage to publish the true figures. There were fewer dead than was originally claimed – 28 rather than 57 – but this number includes 16 children who were killed when the building collapsed on the garage. The toll may be less terrible than we believed – but it is still horrible.

The tragedy at Cana is a turning point. The legitimate war – Israel's act of self defence after Hezbollah's aggression – becomes illegitimate. Israel has become the guilty party and even Condi now says it is time for a ceasefire. Olmert tries to resist the pressure, but is forced to cave in and agree a pause of 48 hours during which there will be no air raids. He witters on that this is not a real ceasefire but just a truce so everyone can get their second wind.

Amir Peretz, the hero of 101 Labour disputes, backs Olmert to the hilt. Now reinvented as a master strategist, Peretz says that 'an immediate cease fire would be a victory for the extremists who would *lift their heads again*'.

I wonder at this turn of phrase. If a ceasefire would allow them to lift up their heads, are we to take it that their heads are currently lowered? Or that Israel has finally damaged Hezbollah's capacity to strike? The expert on strikes – the industrial variety – is, of course, the Minister of Defence who has now acquired the habit of making belligerent statements.

With its head bowed, Hezbollah nevertheless manages to beat its own record, launching 156 rockets into Israel, causing many casualties.

Peretz uses the truce to announce that operations against Hezbollah will intensify. He needs more men, and more reservists are told to report to their units.

It's a point of honour, Peretz declares. He has an answer for everything, He is behaving more and more like a case study from Norman Dixon's *On The Psychology of Military Incompetence*, which dissects a number of disasterous campaigns. In nearly every case, the prime cause of catastrophe was the overconfidence of politicians and generals, and their inability to pay close attention to what was really happening on the battlefield.

July 31

The truce provides a pause for thought, as well as breath.

The press finally begins to use the word *war* and to worry about the strategy. For twenty days, the military experts in the media have almost been playing a TV reality show: *'I am a General, let's get them out of there.'* In their columns and in the TV studios, they assume the all-knowing air of pundits, letting it be understood that commanders are leaking all kinds of interesting and secret tidbits – exclusively to them.

In *The Jerusalem Post*, the editorials are perplexed. Why did the army launch attacks against Bint Jbeil and Maroun-al-Ras, only to retreat after a week of bloody battles? And then why did the commandos go back again?

'The government of Israel thinks that if brute force is not working, the answer is to use *even more force*,' David Grossman notes ironically. 'Military might alone will not bring Israel true security.'

Grossman will eventually set up a pressure group, demanding an immediate ceasefire and the opening of negotiations.

Meanwhile, the young men of the Golani unit change out of their swimsuits, black up their faces and camouflage their caps so that they don't shine at night. This time they go in with tanks and older reservists, but some are still not properly supplied. Some of them march across the border without bullet proof vests, without enough ammunition and without rations. They don't have clear orders either. It is obvious that the army command never contemplated having to call up the reserves.

By the end of the 20th day, 33 soldiers and 51 civilians have been killed in Israel. The death toll in Lebanon is, at least, 589 men, women and children.

Editorial rings to make sure I am still suffering from Stockholm syndrome.

'Have you seen what that coward, *your* Foreign Minister – who also happens to be *our* Foreign Minister – has done now?' They start.

'I know.'

'He thinks that Iran has a major role to play in bringing stability to the region,' they say.

'It's true that the President of Iran is not a natural force for stability,' I reply. 'And Douste knows it, as he's had a taste in Haifa of stabilizing Iranian missiles loaded with 100 kilos of explosive. But maybe there are mitigating circumstances. He was a choir boy in Lourdes, he's got lots of good will and maybe he mistakes his hopes for peace for the reality.'

'You're nuts,' Editorial says. 'It's because Chirac hates the Syrians who killed his friend Hariri.' Hariri, the former Prime Minister of Lebanon, was recently assassinated, and all the evidence pointed to Damascus. 'So Douste must have been told to cosy up to Teheran.'

They treat me as if I am completely ignorant of the ways of French diplomacy.

So we will not speak of a 'stabilizing force', not even to annoy the Syrians. French diplomacy will have to describe it differently.

August 1

'If the Yom Kippur war, in 1973, had also been filmed and on the TV it would have been stopped at once. If we had known how many of our men died every day at the Chinese Farm surrounded by the Egyptians, we would never have pushed on to the Suez Canal,' Katri says. He is now the boss of the Israeli Film Fund. 'Today it's our first war on live TV.'

In 1973, he was in a reconnaissance unit that found the gap between the two Egyptian armies. That gap made it possible for the Israeli army to drive to the Suez Canal.

Katri's commando unit had been sent by Ariel Sharon, a general who believed in Ben Gurion's philosophy of war – a creed of boldness, rapid surprise attacks, lightning strikes and unusual tactics. Israel's first Prime Minister said: 'Everything must be done to get the enemy off guard and give him no time to recover, psychologically or strategically.'

On Yom Kippur, the Egyptians surprised the Israeli army but Sharon's boldness soon turned defeat into victory. He first isolated, then surrounded the Egyptian forces and finally destroyed them in the Sinai desert.

Katri's unit paid a very heavy price. More Israelis died at the battle of Chinese Farm in the Sinai than in the whole war against Hezbollah.

'The difference was that we took the risk of enormous losses in order to strike a major blow and disconcert the enemy,' Katri explains. 'The difference now with this asymmetric war is that the others, our enemies, are willing to die but we have a new war culture here, and that culture demands victory with ZERO DEAD.'

Katri, who also fought in 1967, does not display great confidence in the way the military operated, even when it scattered the Arab armies.

'Sardines,' he tells me. 'I survived thanks to sardines. I always stuffed my pockets with tins of sardines because I knew we would never get any food. And in the end, one of the tins of sardines stopped an enemy bullet.'

There is clearly something very wrong with army catering all over the world. The second best army in the world – the British – are now getting their families to send them food parcels in Iraq. And they don't have enough bulletproof vests, either!

We have dinner at Katri's and watch the comedy show on Channel 10. The producers have invited a Nasrallah lookalike and make jokes about the war. Everyone laughs.

The phone rings while we're eating. Katri, who runs the film fund that has helped finance the new Israeli cinema, hears that a number of international festivals have cancelled screenings of Israeli films.

'The films are critical of Israel and critical of the government, so none of this makes sense,' he complains.

The Edinburgh Film Festival says it will show one Israeli film but would prefer it if the director did not attend. They are 'worried for his safety' and fear that he will be pelted with haggis. The furious director goes to Scotland anyway.

In France, the organisers of the Festival of Lussas show nimble political intelligence, or slavish political correctness. From their native Auvergne, a part of the country best known for its dry sausage, these luminaries think they can deal with the Middle East conflict. They decide to replace the Israeli films with Lebanese and Palestinian ones.

French intellectuals still have some sense, however. A number of writers and film makers, including Costa Gavras, who made a famous film about the Greek colonels (who ousted the democratic government in 1967), send a sharp letter to the festival boss reminding her that it is not very smart to start

134

acting as a censor: 'You think you have made things more balanced,' they write, 'but in fact you have been unbalanced, fuelling misunderstanding and hatred.'

Inevitably, the war affects cultural life. At the Jerusalem Film Festival, Sayed Kashua is on the jury which will award the 'Best Israeli film' prize. At 28 years of age, Sayed is the rising literary and journalistic star among Israeli Arabs. In his funny book, *The Arabs also Dance*, he described his unfunny school days when he could not chat up Jewish girls, was subjected to security checks on the school bus – and did not serve in the army like other young Israeli men. He writes in Hebrew and lives in Tel Aviv.

Sayed was having a good time at the festival when the war started as a mere operation. But the conflict of loyalties gets to him and he describes that very honestly in a piece he writes for the left-ish daily, *Ha'aretz*. It's an emotional shock for his Israeli friends.

'I'm trembling as I write this, but in this war I am against Israel which – please understand – is my country. You could say this is treason, you can say what you want but I am myself baffled. I don't understand why I feel glad when an Israeli tank is hit while at the same time I'm anxious, for some friends of mine may be inside that tank.'

His friends are sad. Furious readers cancel subscriptions to *Ha'aretz* because the daily published a piece which shatters the myth of the Israeli Arab – that he is an *Israeli like every other Israeli*.

The truce is over. With stunning logic Olmert says that Israel has already won.

'Never again will Hezbollah be able to threaten us with its missiles,' he informs Israel's military academy students. Which is why the war has to carry on, it seems. You can never have too much victory.

Another warrior king seems to suffer from this wondrous logic.

Summer Rain

Yes it is none other than our hero of the Stock Exchange, Israel's advocate of let 'death rain from the clouds', 'Wings' Halutz, who has been absent from my diary for a bit. Sorry about that. You will recall that our intrepid top pilot won the war in the first 30 minutes but he has now decided he must win it all over again. So he sends four regiments of infantry, a few thousand soldiers, with tanks to remove all traces of Hezbollah from southern Lebanon.

We are not told how many of these soldiers have taken tins of sardines with them. But we do hear that the battle of Bint Jbeil is still going on. Three more Israelis lose their lives there.

But the reserves are on their way, the army insists.

August 2

I am not doing this on purpose, but I have yet more failures to report.

First failure; the attempt by the elite commandos to capture one of the super-bosses of Hezbollah, Sheikh Mohammed Yazbeck, a special envoy of Iran and a good catch, if he were to be caught.

Yesterday, the Sheikh was admitted to the hospital of Dar al Hikmah in Baalbek, which is in the Beekaa valley, one of Hezbollah's strongholds. The secret services were right about that.

Seeking to restore its super-hero image, the Israeli military commits itself to a spectacular action of the kind that built its reputation.

Let's flashback 30 years, to Entebbe, Uganda, in 1976.

An Air France plane takes off from Tel Aviv and is hijacked by two Palestinians and two Germans. The Popular Front for the Liberation of Palestine has linked up with the German Red Army. The hijackers force the plane to land in Uganda where the bully buffoon, Idi Amin Dada rules. Amin is a former Sergeant in the British army, and an anti-semite. Today, he is best known as the subject of the film *The Last King of Scotland*.

Amin welcomes the hijackers. The hostages are taken to the airport terminal at Entebbe, sorted into groups of Jews and gentiles, and the gentiles are released. The hijackers threaten to shoot all the Jews, unless Israel releases Palestinian prisoners.

The Air France captain, Michel Bacos, shows true heroism. He and his crew will not leave Entebbe unless they leave with all their passengers, he says. So the crew stays with the hostages.

Summer Rain

In 1976, the Israeli military is capable of imagination. Within hours, a daring rescue is plotted, Operation Thunder. The Kenyan government is persuaded to help. An Israeli Hercules, carrying commandos takes off for Entebbe, lands at night with its lights blacked out. A Mercedes, resembling Amin's official car is driven out of the plane: the Ugandan soldiers on the ground assume it is their great leader. Their hesitation gives the Israeli super-commandos time to dash into the terminal and take it. The commandos kill all the hijackers, a few Ugandan soldiers, and free the passengers. The raid takes half an hour; there is one death among the Israelis, that of the commando unit's leader, Yonathan Netanyahu, brother of Binyamin, who will become Israel's Prime Minister 20 years later.

Idi Amin proceeds, without the least embarrassment, to complain to the United Nations about an illegal attack on his country!

Thirty years later, Israel's objective is not to rescue hostages, but to kidnap one single Sheikh. Again at night, helicopters drop 200 soldiers on the hills near Baalbek. One group attacks the Hezbollah Hospital, kills some militia and takes five prisoners. The second group of commandos doesn't do very well. First, it kills a perfectly peaceful Bedouin family sleeping in a tent and then it has to be rescued by the air force.

But the commandos think they have won a terrific victory. They have realised the Sheikh has left the hospital but they've got an even bigger fish; they have captured a man called Hassan Nasrallah, the leader of Hezbollah. It's 1976 all over again.

But in the helicopter the triumphant commanders discover one embarrassing detail. Their prisoner is not *the* Hassan Nasrallah. It is a common Arabic name. There are thousands of them. The man they have is not the Hezbollah leader.

In Tel Aviv, Netanya and Herzliya, the news from Baalbek is not top of the agenda, however. Here the news is that the French have finally turned up. French is now the main language spoken under the parasols on the beach, at the restaurants and in the nightclubs. French Jews, like all French people, go on holiday in August. They have started to arrive in big numbers because they had reservations – and because they did not want to let down their Israeli families and friends.

August 3

In Tel Aviv we recognize the 'People from the North' who have been staying for three weeks in luxury hotels, courtesy of companies like the Delek petrol group and some rich tycoons. The poor don't have flashy luggage and they don't radiate joy; they are weighed down with packages and suitcases; they look more like refugees than holidaymakers.

Many of them look anxious. They're frightened. For their husbands, sons and cousins who have stayed in the north – for the grandmother who stubbornly would not move from her home. All of them are asking the same question – when are we going back home, when are we going to start living normal lives again?

It is very odd to be a refugee in a modern country, but these people are fortunate compared to the Lebanese. Refugees on the other side of the border can't get into their cars and drive away – their roads have been bombed and are badly damaged. Here in Israel, no one is going hungry – apart, bizarrely, from some commandos – and the towns have not been pulverised. But on both sides of the border families have been forced to leave their homes, without knowing where to run to.

Now the war leads to records in terms of how many people one can squeeze into an apartment. I find out how 15 people can sleep in one living room in the smart resort of Herzliya.

Nir Dvir is an energetic young man who works in marketing; he and his wife have two children. They have welcomed his mother-in-law, his brother-in-law with his wife and kids, and his sister-in-law with her husband and children. Mattresses fill the living room and toys are strewn across the floor, but everyone is coping – quite well. The block of flats is built round a communal garden and the kids play outside.

But then a work colleague of Nir's, Yitzik Benamou, turns up – with his wife and their seven children. The three-room flat now creaks at the seams. Yitzik felt they had to leave Nahariya after Hezbollah hit the town with over a hundred rockets.

'We just couldn't stand it any more – the kids were throwing themselves under tables because they were so scared and we had to sleep in the shelter with screaming babies,' he explains.

So Yitzik and his family left Nahariya for Acre – it took two trips, as the family car is not large enough to take the whole family. But wherever they went, the rockets followed, as Hezbollah launched new long-range missiles, which could now hit Acre. Today five people died in the town including a man and a fifteen-year-old girl who came out of the shelter for a few moments to see where the rockets had fallen. Three Arabs were also killed in their village in the Galilee.

These attacks made Yitzik's family take the road to the South. They stayed first with some relatives in Netanya.

'We were seventeen in the appartment, we couldn't take it any more. We were at the end of our tether when Nir suggested we come here,' Yitzik explains.

People in the building get organised. Nir's neighbours make room in their flats for the Benamou family. Everyone eats outdoors, on the lawn.

That evening I tell this tale of improvisation and resilience to Aviva, a friend who runs a Tel Aviv estate agency. She's not surprised.

'I've been sleeping in the living room for the last fifteen days,' she says. 'I've taken in a lady who is 86 and her daughter. I've given them my bedroom because they spend the whole day watching soap operas on TV and it gets on my nerves.'

'Isn't that very hard for you?' I say sympathetically.

'I'm damned if we're going to be beaten by their rockets.'

August 3

I see in *The Jerusalem Post* page upon page of small ads from locals offering shelter to people from the north. The country is enjoying a surge of community spirit; the ultra-orthodox welcome secular Jews into their homes; single people invite large families – and even families with pets – to stay. Young people in Jerusalem and Tel Aviv organize activities and summer camps for young Ethiopians from the North and Arab kids from Galilee. Showbiz stars tour the north to entertain those cooped up in the shelters, some of which don't even have TV.

This surge of community spirit makes everyone forget the very real social and economic divisions in Israel where 25% of the population lives below the poverty line, set at a far from princely level of $426 US a month.

Those social differences hit me forcefully when I go to report on a camp that has sprung up in Nitzanim, near the second front, the border with Gaza.

Those who seek refuge here are refugees in the truest sense. More than 6,000 people are sleeping in huge white tents on the beach under the fierce sun, because they have nowhere else to go.

From a distance it looks like a Club Med resort, because the beach is superb, but up close, the camp is a luxury version of the Palestinian refugee camps a few miles away in Gaza. Every tent houses about 200 people, with huge fans to cool them. The breeze makes the heat more bearable but does not alleviate the overcrowding. Some families string scarves and sheets around their 'spot' to give themselves a modicum of privacy. That is of particular importance to the ultra-orthodox, because their traditions do not allow any contact between men and women. The foam mattresses touch anyway.

The teenagers don't mind this improvised summer camp, especially as superstars descend to give free concerts. The adults feel humiliated and are suffering but they are grateful to a Russian Israeli millionaire, Arcadi Gaydamak, who has provided them with the camp's shelter.

Cometh the crisis, cometh the man. Gaydamak is wanted by the police in France and accused of arms trafficking in Angola, but he has decided to help his fellow citizens. He believed it would be for a week, not a month, and he thought he would be accommodating 2,000 people – not 6,000 or 7,000. This is costing him millions of dollars of his own money.

Gaydamak provides shelter, food, and even entertainment, as well as some security for the campers. He is doing what the State and its institutions are not, and doing it at record speed. In 48 hours, he has managed to set up this canvas village and to arrange water and electricity supplies – there are even sockets where people can recharge their mobile phones. There is also a small amusement park, and a huge stage for shows.

Once he had organised his village, Gaydamak sent busses north to pick up people. They bring the single mothers, the large families, the people who can't afford cars, the poor, the huddled masses.

And they're grateful.

'We had nowhere to go,' they tell me. These exiles in their own country speak with Moroccan, Ethiopian and Ukrainian accents. 'Either we stayed in the shelters or we ventured out and risked being killed by a rocket. It was Russian roulette.'

The Jews have become wanderering Jews again. In the camp, villages re-create themselves; neighbours sit next to one another in the cafeteria, which provides free food.

Everyone waits while they thank Gaydamak for his generosity and efficency. They try not to be depressed by Nasrallah, who can't resist a whoop of triumph when he gives yet another interview from yet another secret location:

'In previous Israeli Arab wars, did you see two million Israelis having to flee and to go into shelters?' Nasrallah exaggerates, which is something of a Middle Eastern tradition. At most a million have fled the North. He also adds, in a piece of wishful thinking, that Israel is a 'provisional country'.

Olmert has no wish to exaggerate the numbers who have

fled the North because the reality already looks bad enough. 'We could not evacuate a million people,' he explains, emphasising the efficiency of the shelters (where he did not have to spend 33 days).

But even here on the sands at Nitzanim, the rockets are a threat. A Qassam launched by Palestinians from Gaza lands in a kindergarten in Ashkelon, at the end of the beach.

The Qassams keep hitting Sderot, the closest town to the border with Gaza. Gaydamak is also the only person to organise holidays in Eilat for the traumatized kids of Sderot. Ironically, the most famous son of Sderot happens to be the heroic Minister of Defence. But Peretz is no better at providing help than he is at organizing defence.

At I leave Gaydamak-City, I pick up a young girl hitchhiking. Unlike the camp's city dwellers she is in neither a bikini nor shorts. She is wearing a long dress and a shirt with sleeves. Strange outfit to wear beneath the blazing sun.

'Where are you going?' I ask her.

She tells me she is going to another improvised town near the motorway. Here there are different kinds of refugees – the ultra-orthodox settlers who were forcibly removed from Gaza so that it could be given back to the Palestinians.

'We were so happy in Gaza,' the girl says. I can hardly believe that she is nostalgic. A few thousand Jews were living in the midst of 1.4 million hostile Palestinians. Jewish homes were surrounded by barbed wire; Jews could only enter and leave their enclave under the protection of the army, using one road surrounded by concrete blocks.

'We had a garden and a lovely house,' says the Orthodox girl, dreaming of moving back to Gaza.

I can't believe what I am hearing. The girl longs to return to Gaza.

August 4

It's Friday. The weekend papers, with their supplements, sell millions of copies. The heavy packet of news is under my arm as I sit at the hotel bar – the authentic war reporter is always to be found in the hotel bar, sipping whisky. But due to yet another lack of decent planning, there is a crisis at the bar of the Nof Hotel. They have run out of lager.

'We had no idea journalists drank so much,' the hotel management says. Have they never seen a war movie?

Ha'aretz has a front page story headlined *Systematic Reverses*, in which they set out the failures of the last 24 days. According to the paper, there has not been one success. Courageously, the paper carries three pages which show how the country is dealing with the war.

I'd like to quote from the brilliant piece by Sayed Kashua, the same young Arab writer, whose earlier article proved so controversial.

Kashua's piece *Sleep Sweet, Pilot Sleep*, starts with brio.

'Wow, I would love being a pilot. If there's one gripe I have about this country, it's that the army was not fair to me when it stopped me being a pilot. Flat feet – that was my problem.'

Flat feet? *Ha'aretz* readers know that it is not his feet that are the problem. Sayed is an Israeli Arab, and thus never to be trusted with a machine gun, let alone an F-16. Sayed, tells readers that he was an ace at video games in his teens and could hit the fastest moving targets. Then he imagines he is a pilot today and writes:

'I am so envious of our pilots in Lebanon. Targets that don't move can also be fun. You line them up in the sights, press the joysticks

147

and that's it. It's a great adrenalin rush, whizzing over the villages and just occasionally dumping a bomb.'

It is when he gets back that Sayed's pilot faces real problems:

'The most dangerous part of it is when you get home after having flown a perfect mission where you hit every target, and the news shows all the children you've killed.'

But hey, maybe it's not my fault, thinks the pilot.

'Anyway... You know they are not like us, they think differently. Do you think those kids just happened to be stuck in that tiny room with disabled people? Well, they locked them in, deliberately, without food or water, hoping an Israeli bomb would wipe them out.'

Ha'aretz publishes this powerful and angry piece in a country where the pilot is a national hero.

But readers grasp that Sayed is an Israeli Arab. The paper goes on to do still better – or worse, depending on your point of view. In the same issue it publishes an article by a soldier called *Why I will go.* And, directly opposite, another soldier's declaration, titled *Why I will not go.*

Yonatan Nir, the one 'who will go', is almost surprised at himself. He remembers crying with joy in 2000, when he was somewhere in the jungles of South America, at the time Israel finally quit Lebanon. Many of his friends had died in Lebanon, uselessly, as he saw it. Now he is in Eilat by the Red Sea when he gets his mobilization orders on the phone. The code is 'Tsav 8'. He has to drop everything. His country needs him.

'Number 5224914 must leave civilian life right now and join the forces fighting in the north. I didn't give it one second's pause. I packed my bags and got the midnight bus from Eilat to Tel Aviv.'

He has all night to consider why he is ready to go and risk his life.

'Travelling towards my unit I hear the same generals and politicians on the radio speaking with their usual confidence and arrogance. I realise I am right to be worried. For these guys the war is their big moment.'

August 4

When he reaches his unit, he realises he has even more to worry about.

'I get a briefing and I understand that what is true today may not be true tomorrow. The man who briefs us recognizes that he is not really sure what was true yesterday... I am given equipment which my father probably used when he crossed the Suez canal in 1973. It stinks so much I suspect it has not been washed since then.

I understand we are in complete chaos and I try out my gun. As I fire at the target I can't stop thinking that a bullet I fire could drill a hole in the skull or body of a woman or a child, and that this bullet could plant another seed of hate in this all-too-hating part of the world.'

So why does he agree to do his duty?

When he got to the bus station in Tel Aviv, there was some graffiti on a dirty wall. It said: *'The Jewish people live.'* But someone had added a question mark. After *'live'*. Nir tells himself he is willing to fight – *because it is a war waged against a group of people who do not want peace at any price.*

The man who says he will not go is Oded Naaman, a philosophy student, who writes from Amsterdam.

'Last week I fled and many people who read this article will say that I became a traitor.'

Oded was already opposed to Operation Summer Rain.

'It was clear to me that bombing a civilian population could not be a proper price to pay in order to obtain security for people living in Sderot. After the capture of Shalit and the return of our soldiers to Gaza, I understood that it was not worth even trying to imagine a logical solution to this mess.'

At 19.00 on July 21, a friend in his unit rings Oded to say there is a rumour that they will get their mobilisation orders on Sunday.

I could not sleep that night, Oded writes.

Oded phones his parents and tells them he will not go. He knows the consequences – he will get a criminal record and be put in jail. His uncle suggests that he should leave at once with him and fly to the Netherlands. A loophole in the law concerning military service says that if you are abroad when you get your orders to report to your unit, failure to report for duty is not a crime.

As soon as Oded gets off the plane in Amsterdam, his mobile phone rings. It is the army, but his orders have arrived too late. He is beyond their grasp.

'I do not think it is legitimate to ask the citizens of a country to sacrifice their lives without proper reasons. And slogans such as 'we need to use force to dissuade them' and 'humiliation of the army' are not good enough. That is just militant patriotism. I fled and perhaps became a traitor because I want to finish my exams rather than die to bolster the egos of our generals.'

Israel's free press is one of its glories. You can really say anything here and many criticisims of Israel by Israelis would be considered extreme by some British and American audiences. It is the start of a major national self-analysis.

August 5

Today, Israel's communists are on the march. I had never seen a red flag or communist demo in the streets of Tel Aviv or Jerusalem.

When a friend rings to tell me of the first demonstration against the second Lebanon war, I grab my reporter's notebook and head towards the old center of Tel Aviv.

It's a disappointment – journalistically. There are many policemen, and very few genuine demonstrators. Those that have turned up are unimpressive – a few dishevelled folk who seem to have come out of mothballs and clench their fists in a communist salute. The crowd consists of a few Jews, and not even that many Israeli Arabs. There is no sense whatever of a groundswell against the war.

'You can say,' I tell Alex as I ring him at his agency, 'that this is a wash-out. A few hundred demonstrators, most of them militant commies.'

'You're sure? Not even a thousand?' Alex sounds worried before he writes his story, which will fly round the world.

'I am quite sure. It is a mini-demo of minimalist proportions – of commies and a few Israeli Arabs. It is not a mass movement against the war,' I tell him.

Alex writes his story, confident that the demo was a damp squib. His reward is a number of outraged phone calls from the police and insults from the militants. Both are angry that he has not bought into their inflated figures of the numbers of demonstrators.

I put my reporter's notebook away seconds before Yael Dayan, daughter of the famous one-eyed general Moshe Dayan, gets

151

up on the platform. She is something of a political celebrity herself, very feminist, very left-wing, and currently holds the office of Deputy Mayor of Tel Aviv. She makes it clear that she is not speaking for Peace Now, the movement set up in 1982 to stop the first Lebanon war. Since the Operation against Hezbollah started, the left and Peace Now have supported the government – like everyone else.

'Yes, I was for this war at the start because it started as a war in which we were defending ourselves and I have not come here to speak against Tsahal,' Yael Dayan says.

Tsahal, the name for the army, makes the small crowd go wild. People start to whistle and scream. Some men come close to her podium throwing cans of soft drinks at her.

Yael Dayan looks small and fragile but she is not intimidated. 'We in the Peace Now movement are not against the army, and not even against the government, but I think we must stop this military offensive and not intensify it,' she says loudly into the mike.

No one listens to her. The demonstrators whistle and hoot. She gets off the platform, protected by some burly men. The police offer to escort her safely away. She refuses, shrugging her shoulders as if to say 'what will happen will happen'.

I grab my notebook and go to talk to her.

'We need a ceasefire on both sides,' she tells me. 'Someone in authority must say "stop". We have to negotiate a permanent deal with the Lebanese government – and also with Syria. Our soldiers have to come out of Lebanon and an international force must replace them – and the Lebanese army too. And we must get our kidnapped soldiers back.' But she is not typical of Peace Now. Most pacifists still support the government.

Cartoons in the papers make fun of these Peaceniks who have turned their flowers into swords. One shows a typical Peace Now member with long hair sipping his capucccino on the terrace of a Tel Aviv café. 'We won't stop till we have wiped Beirut off the map!' he says...

August 5

To get a better sense of the mood among the left, I contact Motti Raz. He is forty years old and the former leader of Peace Now. Earlier this year he was elected to the Knesset as a member for Yossi Beilin's left-wing Meretz-Yachad group. I am expecting to interview a pacifist, so I am a bit surprised when he informs me he is in his paratrooper uniform.

'Yes, I am at the front. Obviously I can't tell you where I am precisely for reasons of security. I'm not glad to be here, but I live in a democratic country, which has the right to call me up. Luckily I have not committed any criminal act, I have not shot anyone as I'm too old to be in the heart of the fighting.'

Even though he is in uniform, even though he is with other soldiers, he does not have any problem in saying what he thinks of the army and the government.

'Israel was attacked by a terrorist organisation and we have every right to defend ourselves, but this government has not conducted this war intelligently and it should stop now. It's not a question of ethics but of efficency. When in October 2000, Ehud Barak had to deal with the crisis of soldiers who had been kidnapped, he responded with a quick operation and then stopped. It was smarter.'

Then the peacenik paratrooper says goodbye and goes to rejoin his unit somewhere at the front.

The few critical voices have a negligible impact on public opinion. We have military and verbal escalation. Shimon Peres, winner of the Nobel Peace Prize, announces that the war is not yet finished. 'And it is not a matter of days but of weeks.'

I am not sure he believes that himself. He knows that France and the United States are putting the final touches to a ceasefire resolution they will present to the Security Council in a matter of days.

So is Peres bluffing? Does it all come down to a question of honour now, that honour which obsesses the military in every culture?

Or is it just, as David Grossman has said, that when the

153

military chiefs see that force is not working, they send in even more force.

If the sledgehammer won't crack the nut, hit it with a laser-guided missile.

August 6

Today the great and good of Israel try to intervene. The three greatest living Israeli novelists, who are often seen as the moral guardians of the country, take out their pens and cheque books. Amos Oz, A.B Yehoshua and David Grossman buy a full-page ad in *Ha'aretz* to express their opposition to the government's escalation, which has just announced it will send more troops into Lebanon.

The writers plead for an immediate ceasefire and an immediate stop to all attacks on Lebanon. They remind readers that they all supported the war when it began:

The war started off as legitimate and was inevitable. But it has succeeded to some extent and it is no longer legitimate. Continued military action is no longer in Israel's best interest. No more blood must be spilt on either side.

The political class does not respond and the public are all for carrying on till the job is done. They have been made very aware of the danger of an armed Hezbollah on their doorstep.

Hezbollah is not keen to stop the war either. 'We refuse the project of the resolution of the UN which is against the interests of the Lebanon,' says Nabih Berri, Lebanon's Prime Minister.

'We will only stop fighting when there is not a single Israeli soldier on Lebanese soil,' declares one of the leaders of Hezbollah, who is also a Minister in the Lebanese government.

But it is the Syrian Foreign Minister who dangles the reddest of rags. 'We are ready for a regional war,' he trumpets on a visit to Beirut. This war hasn't been big enough for him. A regional war is welcome.

So blood continues to flow, Jewish blood, Arab blood, Israeli

155

blood, Palestinian blood, Hezbollah blood, Lebanese blood, Hamas blood.

The Israeli air force continues to bomb Beirut, Tyre, Baalbek, and the bridges across the Litani River, where convoys carrying humanitarian aid cross into the south.

And today Hezbollah hits the jackpot. One rocket blasts into a group of reserve paratroopers sitting on the lawn of a kibbutz. They were preparing to leave for the front. One ultra-orthodox Jew dies with his skullcap on his head, by the side of a hippie with pierced ears and a recent Ukrainian immigrant. In all, twelve reservists who had just left their normal civilian lives die on the lawn.

August 7

Reuters has been exposed – and has caved in.

A very matter of fact wire from the agency tells us that it is withdrawing from its library *all the photos* taken by Adnan Hajj, who liked to embellish his pictures. For Hajj there was just not enough smoke spewing out of the craters left by Israeli bombs; he felt it was artistically necessary to add more plumes of white trailing from the F-16s over the Lebanon sky.

Yet the reality, the true truth, is frightening enough.

Reuters is forced to withdraw the pictures because meticulous bloggers prove that they have been rather crudely retouched. That becomes obvious when you look carefully at the *before* and *after* photos. But Reuters did not like to admit it – no doubt to protect its reputation.

'The picture was not deliberately manipulated, the photographer Adjan said he had tried to clean up some traces of *dust* on the negative,' the Reuters spokeswoman says, without a trace of irony. How can cleaning up a picture involve adding a big cloud of black dust to the Beirut sky?

The second statement informs us that Reuters withdraws its previous statement and adds that it has now also cleaned up its stock of images – and removed all trace of these doctored negatives.

The Internet is full of control freaks who patrol the IT waves. Those who want to fake images are going to have to control themselves. The whole world is watching the media war.

But the war now creates an utterly surreal photo-op.

Tonight TV cameras have taken over the old harbour of Tel Aviv with its flashy bars and exclusive restaurants. The lenses are trained on people dressed to the nines. I imagine I've stumbled on some kind of reality show.

But the image is arresting – it seems to be a gathering of couples and newlyweds. I quickly learn what is going on; collateral damage of the matrimonial kind. As a result of Hezbollah's rockets, weddings have had to be cancelled all over northern Israel, because nobody wants to see one of Stalin's Organs crashing into their wedding cake. Sort of ruins the day.

A young cinema producer, Eliman Bardugo – himself to be married soon – hit on the idea of a gigantic mass marriage ceremony where all those who had to cancel their weddings could get hitched. The beach at Tel Aviv is now the scene of a fifty couple wedding fiesta.

Tonight, it is not the military that's going into action, but Israel's finest dressmakers, hairdressers, make-up artists, florists, caterers and photographers. The aim is to provide an unforgettable experience for the hundred newlyweds and their rabbis, families and friends. People are working for free. The celebrations seem to be a big success, though I didn't spend the night at the harbour.

There were apparently no just before they said 'I do' dramas – everybody got married and married to the right person or, at least, the person they had come with. No one tried to change partners at the last minute.

August 8

At dawn, Jil rings from Paris.

'What do you think of the situation?" she asks.

'It is not very clear,' I reply.

'Okay, you're going to explain it to me, live, in three minutes,' Jil orders.

'That things aren't clear?'

'Maybe you can stretch it to five minutes. I'll call at 7.59.'

She hangs up.

I write out two columns – one for good news and one for bad.

Jil rings back on the dot at 7.59 and launches into 'and here we have the up to date analysis from *Libération*'s special correspondent *at the front*.'

'Today I'm not at the front,' I point out.

'You were there yesterday,' she snaps.

'Okay, well I am *live in Tel Aviv*, with good news and bad news. Given that the region is not known for good news it's amazing we have some. The Lebanese government is ready to send 15,000 troops to southern Lebanon with the support of the United Nations peacekeepers. The aim is to take back some control of *Hezbollahland*. Everyone is happy. Nasrallah knows the Lebanese soldiers are less likely to give him trouble than the international peacekeepers. And the Security Council seems close to agreeing terms for a ceasefire.'

The day also brings bad news. The bombing of Beirut and south Lebanon has killed thirty more civilians. The battle of Bint Jbeil is still going on and Hezbollah has now reached a new record of 140 rockets launched against northern Israel in one day. Finally – and I don't know whether it is good news or bad – Nasrallah, the head of Hezbollah, has said to the Arabs in Haifa: 'We have been saddened by your martyrs and your wounded, I beg you to leave the town.'

The list of the martyrs who sadden Nasrallah, the lachrymose leader, is getting longer.

Fadia Jumaa and her two daughters, Samira and Sultana, were killed by his rockets in the Arab village of al-Aramshe in the Galilee. The Arabs have no families living further south who can take them in, so they have to stay at home.

Nasrallah has claimed that his capacity to strike is not affected,' Jil adds. 'Is there a real threat to Haifa?' She adds: 'Is this is bluff, or is it propaganda?'

'In any case the Israelis hit a Hezbollah drone and it's fallen over the sea,' I say. 'On its way to...'

'A drone?' Jil asks. Like me, she has the disadvantage of not having studied for a Master in Missiles.

'A plane with no pilot. It is a level more sophisticated than missiles and other rockets. It's a question of super-technology,' I explain to the listeners. 'It's a kamikaze full of explosive – but without the kamikaze pilot.'

'And finally,' Jil asks, 'do you think the ceasefire will happen soon?'

'Yes, Israel and Hezbollah both know they can't win this war and neither has lost it. Yet.'

August 9

The Olmert government has voted for war. More war, to be waged at top speed – before the Americans and the French get a ceasefire resolution through the Security Council.

The Israeli military plan is hardly original. To storm to the Litani River, destroy the rocket launchers, and push the enemy away from the border.

In the Cabinet everyone votes to support the plan, but there are three abstentions. One of the abstainers is Shimon Peres, who finally thinks diplomacy should be given a chance.

Olmert waits for the Security Council to meet before giving the order to attack. But the army, with its tanks and trucks now can't wait, and is already rolling towards the border. There are busses full of reservists and also empty busses – ready to bring the reservists back – when they are tired. And traumatized.

This Wednesday will turn out to be a day of disaster for the reservists and a catastrophe for the military chiefs. Soldiers of any honour would have resigned. A government of honourable men and women would have resigned.

On the battlefield the disasters start early. During the night, the Nahal brigade and a column of tanks enter Lebanon and head for the village of Al Taibeh; they reach it at about 8 a.m.

At the same time, reservists of the 226 Brigade are already there. Their orders are to ambush Hezbollah. These men are lucky to be alive; they are part of the unit that was hit on the kibbutz lawn at Kfir Giladi where twelve of their comrades were killed.

When it comes to ambushes, the real specialists are Hezbollah who know every corner, every stone and every hiding place in the villages of South Lebanon. They have spent six years preparing for this war.

What happens next seems comic, but it ends up as no laughing matter: the two groups of Israeli soldiers *do not know* that they are both on the same road – at the same time in the same place. The question is, exactly what did the commander of the Northern Region know?

Soldiers of the Nahal Brigade see men who are hiding – the very paratroopers who are preparing to ambush Hezbollah.

But, somehow, they don't recognise their comrades in arms. *'Hezbollah fighters,'* proclaims the leader of the 226 Brigade.

He orders a tank to open fire. The order is carried out. One Israeli reservist dies in this friendly fire incident and seven men are wounded.

The official army explanation is a triumph of P.R only P.R now stands for Perfectly Ridiculous: 'The error is the result of a *failure* of coordination of the movements of troops in the area,' the military communiqué announces.

Three hours later, more 'failures'. A Kornet missile hits a Merkava tank. The best tank in the world is not strong enough and four men die.

Their comrades can't save the tank crew. Again, the official explanation would be laughable if it did not bring tears for the dead. 'First Hezbollah are using *modern* missiles,' complains the Israeli army. To make things worse, the tank's fire extinguisher system – the sprinkler system – was not working.

It seems that our military geniuses in intelligence did not know, or, at least, did not reveal, to the army the fact that the Syrians have supplied Russian missiles to Hezbollah. But then, one can hardly expect an army that does not manage to provide rations for its men to keep its fire fighting equipment in trim.

At 1 p.m. there is another disaster. Hezbollah fire a missile at a house in which there are many reservists and soldiers from one of the elite units. The house collapses; the soldiers are buried. Nine reservists die. The army struggles to extricate all the soldiers from the rubble. In the evening, another reservist is killed by a mortar.

Despite all this, many of these non-professional soldiers are proud to be reservists and to defend their country. A friend of mine explains that when her husband (who is a Professor) gets his mobilization orders, she locks the door of their flat so he can't leave. But he goes out through a window, runs into the garden and joins his comrades.

This is a war fought by one of the most voluble democracies in the world. Israelis may come from all corners of the earth but they share one trait. It is a proud tradition of Judaism that men can question God. If you can cross examine the Lord of Hosts you won't feel intimidated by generals. The reservists return from the Lebanon appalled by the incompetence of their leaders and start to speak out.

For one thing, the reservists were sent in without proper training – only a week for those who were not in the elite squads. I have already reported how many of them had old equipment. It now emerges that some units received contradictory orders, or no orders at all. One unit claims they did not move from their camp on a hilltop and had a grandstand view of exchanges of fire overhead for days.

'They forgot us,' these reservists said to themselves.

Possibly.

Other reservists sat waiting in tanks which were not moving and, therefore, extremely vulnerable. The tank crews soon discovered that budget cuts had dispensed with the equipment that sent up smokescreens and counter-measures to hide them from the enemy.

And the Minister of Defence had not purchased the Shield of David, a sophisticated radar system, which could have detected incoming missiles and pinpointed exactly where they came from. Peretz had also stopped developing the Nautilus system, a laser shield based on American technology which can destroy anti-tank missiles in flight. The Patriot anti-missile warhead, which was so useful when Saddam fired Scuds at Israel in 1991, is no longer state of the art because it hits missiles when they are flying quite low.

The reality is that Israel did not understand its enemy. The army saw Hezbollah as a rag-tag militia, not as a proper organisation with modern technology at its disposal. Now, as if they don't have enough troubles, Israeli soldiers face a problem common to celebrities worldwide. Their phones are being hacked. Not by the tabloids, but by Hezbollah, who listen in when Israeli soldiers call home. Being Jewish boys, they are apt to tell their mothers everything – including where they are. And the Jewish mothers keep on calling their sons to see if they are safe, and eating properly. The army eventually has to confiscate all mobile phones.

Hezbollah does not use mobile phones, but relies on couriers who criss-cross the combat zone on Vespas. As for Bin Laden, he relies on carrier pigeons.

I meet Igor, a hard man of the Alexandroni brigade. He ripples with muscles and has more tattoos than a convict. The man looks a bit like a tough nut Hollywood hero. He was born in the Ukraine and works as a lawyer in Tel Aviv.

After the ceasefire, Igor leads a revolt by reservists who camp out for weeks under the windows of the Prime Minister's office and the Knesset in Jerusalem. Their demand is simple – they want the heads of the three men they see as responsible for this fiasco – Olmert, Peretz and Halutz.

'Our leaders mobilized 30,000 reservists and had no idea how to use them,' Igor complains after two weeks in the Lebanon. 'Army HQ took incoherent decisions. They ordered a unit up to the border and then told them to scuttle back. It is normal for people to die in a war but it is not normal for soldiers to go into action without food or water.'

'Did you see Hezbollah close up?' I ask.

'Yes, I saw their men. They shot at us from the villages and hid among civilians. We fought hand to hand. They're good

164

fighters, but not as good as we are. At the Alexandroni brigade we are well trained. I work out every day to stay fit. And no one in my unit has any morale problem. If we're called up again we'll all go back again – no question. We are all friends and this is our only country. We did good work but we would have done much better – and the worse thing is that we did not manage to free our kidnapped soldiers.'

August 10

The pen is mightier than the sword is not a maxim that applies in Jerusalem these days.

The advertisement by Israel's three great writers in *Ha'aretz* did not stop the war. The government voted to keep on fighting this Thursday, so yet again the writers drop their novels in progress and go into political action.

Amos Oz, David Grossman and A. B. Yehoshua summon journalists to a press conference in Tel Aviv in a hall opposite the Defence Ministry. They hope to be the voices of reason and to be heard at home and abroad.

'We have already gone twice to the Litani River,' Yehoshua starts, 'so there does seem to be little point in going back there a third time. The Lebanese Prime Minister is finally suggesting that he will deploy his army down to the border so we must not miss out on this opportunity. Lebanon will always be our neighbour. This is not like Vietnam for the Americans and that's why we have to treat the Lebanese with consideration. Let's not destroy them. We need to pick up the talks with the Palestinians while the war carries on in Lebanon.'

'The spiral of hate that militant Islamic extremists want to foster is different from what is happening in the conflict between Israel and the Palestinians,' Amoz Oz continues. 'This war is a means by which Iran, using Hezbollah, is trying to see if it can wreck Israeli society with one provocation after another. To imagine we are going to win against the Axis of Evil, change the Middle East and create a new Lebanon is an illusion. Israel needs to settle for less ambitious aims and do our best to *limit* the influence of evil forces, rather than to hope to destroy them.'

167

'Israel has exhausted its right to self defence,' says David Grossman. 'The force we are using now only fans the flames of hatred against us in the region and in the world. If the Lebanese Prime Minister had offered to deploy his army on the border a month ago we would have leapt with joy. We will never have a better offer, even if we smash the whole of the Lebanon to bits. It's absurd – and a lie – to claim that if we have our army on the Litani, the Hezbollah rockets will stop. Hezbollah wants us to get more and more entangled in the Lebanon quagmire because then Lebanon will collapse and Hezbollah will be able to take power. That catastrophic scenario can still be avoided now.'

None of us had any idea how bitterly ironic David Grossman's talk of a 'catastrophic scenario' would turn out to be.

Having given their press conference, the three writers leave the building and cross the road to join a demonstration against the war outside the Ministry of Defence. The demonstration has been organised by the ultra-left and Peace Now. But the country is not interested. There are just a few hundred protestors – mainly old time pacifists and a few young hippies. They manage to disrupt the traffic with their placards, but get absolutely no sympathy from drivers, who are annoyed that the demo causes a major traffic jam.

By the 30th day, the death toll in the Lebanon reaches above 1,000. I cannot count the dead among the Party of God because it remains elusive – in every sense. They disappear into the hills and villages and never say how many of their men have died.

On the Israeli side, 38 civilians have died and 81 soldiers.

Today Hezbollah shatters another record as it launches 65 rockets. In the Galilee they hit the Arab village of Dir al Assad. A young teacher, Miriam Assadi, is killed along with her five-year-old son, Fathi. The missile smashes into their house and explodes in the kitchen. Miriam's other little boy, three-year-old Faris, survives, as well his grandmother, but the toddler has to have his leg amputated.

August 11

The stubborn efforts of the French boy scout and Foreign Minister, who soldiered on, despite being ridiculed in the press and obstructed by the Elysée Palace, begin to show results. So does the pressure Condoleeza Rice applies to the warring parties. Condi and the Boy Scout finally succeed in drafting what must be a good ceasefire resolution, because neither side is entirely happy with it.

I have to congratulate French diplomacy and the United Nations which, for once, has done something useful. The fifteen members of the Security Council vote unanimously for resolution 1701 which requires an *immediate end to all hostilities*. Hezbollah must cease its attacks and Israel must stop all offensive military actions.

The unusually helpful members of the United Nations agree to send 15,000 peacekeepers to help the Lebanese army restore order in southern Lebanon. The fate of the kidnapped soldiers is mentioned but there is nothing in the resolution to oblige Hamas and Hezbollah to hand them over.

And then?

Condoleeza Rice picks up the phone and rings the Prime Minister of Lebanon. Fouad Sinoura says that he accepts the resolution and that his government will vote on it that Saturday.

Then she rings the Prime Minister of Israel. 'I support the resolution,' says Ehud Olmert, 'and my government will vote on Sunday but there is no question of our stopping for now.'

Then he gives his military chiefs the green light. Their aim is to steamroller across the border up to the Litani. Israel also keeps sending in the planes and hitting the wrong targets. An

Israeli drone fires on a convoy of fleeing civilians, and seven people are killed. A jet destroys a bridge – 12 people die. The army says it has taken the precaution of dropping leaflets, warning the population to leave. It then bombs all the roads and bridges by which they might be able to escape.

Hezbollah does not comment on the United Nations Resolution but keeps launching missiles and more missiles.

Condoleeza Rice is being quite realistic, just in case the Security Council gets too enthusiastic about Resolution 1701.

'We can't hope that a Resolution will end all the violence,' she explains. 'We must ask all the states in the region and especially Iran and Syria to respect the sovereignty of the Lebanese government and the wishes of the international community. Hezbollah and its sponsors have brought devastation on the Lebanese people, dragging them into a war they did not choose and using them as a human shield.'

Resolution or no resolution, Hezbollah remains elusive. Its sponsors have armed it to the teeth and it melts into the countryside.

Resolution 1701 is hardly any better than Resolution 1559, which was voted in 2004. That called on all foreign forces to leave Lebanon and demanded that all guerilla groups be disarmed. None of that happened.

The United Nations Plaza in Manhattan, where the UN cooks up its resolutions, is far from the Middle East. And words are only words – even if 15,000 UN Peacekeepers are on the way.

'On paper it's a good deal,' writes Nahum Barnea, a very lucid political commentator. 'It promises the disarmament of Hezbollah, that its forces move north, that a proper multinational force takes its place to check who goes in and who goes out of Lebanon. Our kidnapped soldiers should be freed. But you'd need to be a chronic optimist to think people will stick to this deal.'

It is too soon to rejoice. The war goes into a final high-speed frenzy.

August 11

This evening I go to dinner at Hanna Azoulay Hasfari's house; she is a famous actress here. Shabbat dinner is anxious. Her 18-year-old son, Arie, has just finished his training as a conscript during which he marched through the desert with 40 kilos on his back. Arie is an artist and musician, part of Tel Aviv's golden or decadent youth. But he has chosen to do his military service in a combat unit like his father did. He is an artillery gunner and could be sent to Lebanon in the next few hours. The family freezes every time the phone rings while we eat. It could be the army ordering Arie into action.

Arie's father, Shmuel, a playwright, gets home. He is out of breath and covered with dust. He has come back from the front though he did not go to fight. He is too old for active duty, and seems to regret that.

'I wanted to smell the smell of war,' he tells me, 'so I took my car and drove up the front. It was Hell. Tanks and guns on the road, an endless rain of rockets on the towns, everything burning. In 1982 when I was fighting, I left from Metulla to cross into Lebanon. The smell's the same now.'

'What is the point of sending all these soldiers across the border when the ceasefire will come into operation in three days?' I ask.

'No point at all,' he replies.

He is right.

August 12

The 32nd day of the war is a very black day.

We now know that the first round of Hezbollah versus Israel will end the day after tomorrow. The result is that both sides go into overdrive in a desperate attempt to 'look' like the winner.

'Wings' Halutz is about to bid for place in the pantheon of generals who ignored intelligence, looked the wrong way and ended up not just beaten – but ridiculed. His government has just voted for a ceasefire and now he asks – and gets permission – to launch a massive strike into Lebanon.

'The operation will take a week and will make a lasting impression,' Halutz announces, oblivious to the fact that the government has agreed the ceasefire will start in 48 hours.

A very lasting impression on whom? Nasrallah? Conquering 30 kilometres of Hezbollah-land only to have to retreat in about 48 hours is another strategy of genius. Nasrallah will just wait for the ceasefire and then stroll back across the Litani.

The Israeli Armada is dusted down out of mothballs and sent into action to conquer these thirty kilometres. It becomes the largest paratroop operation since the 1973 war. Tanks trundle along the roads, soldiers come down from the hills. It is like a brilliant Hollywood production of a war epic.

By the afternoon the army reaches the Litani River, to make itself believe that it has achieved its goal. Hezbollah has been dealt with.

Not quite!

'Hezbollah has only used ten per cent of its arsenal,' boasts the Hezbollah leadership.

If they are telling the truth, then the sums are like this:
Missiles launched at Israel: 3,700.
Total Missile Stock: 37,000.
Still available to launch: 33,300 missiles.

Hezbollah will be re-supplied by its sponsors, Iran and Syria. Iran now has rockets with a range of 2,000 kilometres, so if the mullahs also want to hit Athens, there is nothing to stop them. Hezbollah also bolsters its position in Lebanon by giving every Shiite family 10,000 Iranian dollars. As a result, the actual government of Lebanon is more and more like a hostage in its own land.

When the fighting stops, the baker, the butcher and the pharmacist will bury their arms, wash their Hezbollah uniforms and go back to work. I am reminded of Mao's maxim that a good guerilla is like a fish in water, part of the landscape. Even more so when I see a picture published in an Australian paper. Photographers have been threatened with death if they take pictures of Hezbollah's weapons but one has managed to get a very striking image. It's like a village fete. A number of happy guerillas sit on a small truck parked in a courtyard. People look out of their windows. There is a rocket launcher on the truck. The smiling guerillas are ready to fire.

The *lasting impression* Halutz was so keen on making reminds me of other wars, like Vietnam. To beat the enemy, the army used cluster bombs, which sprinkle smaller bombs when they detonate. Small cylinders of explosives will litter the fields and roads for years. Humanitarian organisations believe that both Israel and Hezbollah have used thousands of these weapons. Inevitably, in the months to come, a child, a farmer or a mother will tread on one of these unexploded bombs. With luck, they will only lose a leg.

These cluster bombs don't just contravene international law; their use contravenes the Israeli army's own rules of engagement. The high command professes itself to be baffled that these were used at all. On their orders? It wasn't me, sir. It was another general or some over-enthusiastic colonel.

August 12

Halutz now orders an immediate inquiry into how this happened on his watch.

'I am not surprised but I am disappointed,' he says.

Halutz is an exception. For the last 32 days, most of the Israeli population has believed the army when it denied reports that these illegal weapons were being used.

On Saturday, the day before the ceasefire, the air force carries on bombing, almost blindly. It kills 15 people in the village of Rshef, 5 kilometres from the border.

This demonstration of power, however, also brings losses. An Israeli helicopter is shot down and five people die on board. Hezbollah has got hold of new effective anti-tank weapons which can pierce the Merkava tanks. It's classic – everyone is using the last day of the war to try out their latest weapons.

Joseph, the young commando from the Golani I interviewed, has returned to fight in Lebanon in spite of his fear.

'In the village of Shakif al Amal one of our tanks was going in reverse, ' he is still shaking as he speaks. 'The tank crew did not see our comrades who were asleep on the ground. It crushed two men in my unit to death and two others were injured.'

The army announces triumphantly that it has killed forty Hezbollah fighters. But it has to admit, less triumphantly, that it lost twenty-four men this Shabbat.

As has happened every day, the papers publish the name of every soldier who has died this Saturday – with one exception.

August 13

In 24 hours it will all be over. But meanwhile, nothing stops.

Israeli journalists embedded with the army speak of the absurdity of this war, which is being waged until the very last minute.

The journalists have just spent the night with the 162nd Division. Their mission: to take Wadi Saluki and other small villages close to the Litani. To do that, they have to climb a 400-metre hill.

Hezbollah is waiting for them. The commander's tank hits a mine. Ten other tanks are hit by Hezbollah's new anti-tank shells and burst into flame. The soldiers try to take refuge in a grove of olive trees.

By dawn, under fire from Hezbollah, they have reached the top of the hill. Then they get the order from Army Headquarters 'Stop. Mission terminated. Do not move.'

Twelve soldiers have died to take this useless hill.

'Why did these soldiers die?' The journalists ask.

'Our comrades died for nothing,' the reservists say.

In the last 48 hours of the war, 33 soldiers are killed in the dash for the Litani river. 'They died for the egos of the government of non-military men who wanted to prove they had balls,' my friend Alex says.

The ceasefire is approved. It will come into force at 8 a.m. tomorrow. With its modern communications, the Israeli army should be able to order its troops to stop fighting, but how will Hezbollah get word to all its fighters? By Vespa? By carrier pigeon?

Alex heads north. 'I want to hear the silence,' he tells me.

177

He is not really convinced that there is going to be peace, which is why he takes his helmet and bullet-proof vest with him.

'You may hear the silence but you won't see anything, because as usual everything is going on the other side of the border,' I tell him.

'It is a mystical experience – suddenly no more gunfire, a clear blue sky...'

I hesitate about going with him because I can't quite sell myself on this historic mystical experience. I suspect that a few kilometers from the front line there will be a traffic jam and that I will be stuck behind military vehicles and American TV trucks trying to commandeer the best camera positions.

But I finally decide to make the trip, even though I am not properly equipped – I still don't have a bullet-proof vest – when the phone rings. It's Shlomo Papirblatt, the editor of *Yedioth*, and he is desperately upset.

'You know who was the 24th soldier to die yesterday, the man we did not name?' he starts.

'No.'

'No one could reach his brother, who is somewhere in South America, and the rule is that you do not publish until all members of the family know.'

It is clear that another member of a tank crew has died. But his identity is a shock.

'It's the son of David Grossman,' Shlomo tells me.

Two days after his father, together with Amos Oz and A.B. Yehoshua, called for an immediate stop to the war, Uri Grossman was killed in his tank.

His death will become more 'famous' than the deaths of the other 23 who died today. It is a real symbol of this tragedy. Uri's father fought as hard as he could to get a ceasefire – for the sake of Israel – and now he has lost his son. The whole country will mourn with him. The Grossman family issues a statement later in the day, together with a photograph of Uri, a smiling young man, who looked remarkably like his father. The statement reads:

'Uri would have celebrated his 21st birthday in two weeks. He had joined "the cavalry" and achieved his dream of being a tank commander. He was going to finish his military service in November, go travelling all over the world and then study theatre. On Friday he rang us from Lebanon. He spoke to his parents and to his sister. He was happy that there was going to be a ceasefire and promised that he was coming home for dinner on Friday.'

The Grossman family are inundated with messages of sympathy from Israel and around the world.

August 14

Noemi, my filmmaker friend, and I have decided to opt for a TV breakfast, to watch the ceasefire live at 8 a.m. We're sitting in front of a pot of coffee as we watch the count down begin. Thirty minutes to go, twenty minutes, ten...

The atmosphere is reminiscent of New Year, the World Cup Final or the Superbowl. The TV stations have sold premium spots, for deodorants, beer and bubble bath ads. The screen is full of half-naked women. The early morning is prime-time today, with the whole population of Israel glued to its TV screens.

Between the ads, we see the front where the last rockets are still whizzing through the sky to and from the border. People will die until the last second of this war.

Alex rings me from the HQ of Northern Command. 'We've had rockets and artillery all night, people are wondering if this ceasefire will kick in – never mind hold.'

Jil calls to consult the Oracle – me – for her radio station.

'Can you tell us if the fighting will stop?'

'I think so, but let's speak after 8 a.m,' the Oracle declares.

With 5 minutes to go, Israeli TV shows an officer on a field telephone. It is clamped to his ear. He awaits The Order.

On the stroke of 8 a.m., he smiles and signals 'Okay!' It's a thumbs-up. The shooting stops immediately. The soldiers hug each other and throw off their helmets.

But no one applauds as the curtain falls. The end of the war is a non-event. Cameras film the sky, which is suddenly hushed and empty.

'We can hear the birds, which is really strange,' says my new cousin from kibbutz Hanita. He is walking quietly towards the border with his mobile in his hand. He wants me to share the experience.

At 8 a.m. sharp, Hezbollah fighters tidy away their missiles and rocket launchers. No breakaway group decides to risk firing one last Organ of Stalin at the Zionist entity. Not one shot comes from their side. They are a disciplined army, and as organised as Hell.

Noemi's phone keeps on ringing. Parents breathe sighs of relief because their children will not have to go to war, but not all the phone calls are joyful. Friends ring to tell her the time of burials, because some of the soldiers who died in the last two days were sons of friends or colleagues.

Seconds after the ceasefire begins, exhausted reservists climb out of their tanks. Without waiting to change into civilian clothes, they go in front of the cameras to explain the war was a complete waste of time, effort and lives.

'Our comrades have died for nothing,' they say, their faces still blacked up as they accuse the military, the Ministry of Defence and the government of total incompetence.

'And our kidnapped soldiers are still being held,' they point out.

'This is Israel,' says Noemi, 'everyone will soon be at everyone else's throat. There will be commissions of inquiry and reports but today it is more serious. We have suffered a moral crisis. It's *a political earthquake.*'

Still, Ehud Olmert is in a good mood.

'The military offensive has *eliminated* Hezbollah's state within the state of Lebanon,' he claims. This is simply untrue. It is more likely that Olmert will be *eliminated* politically. Despite the last minute gallop to the Litani, which was supposed to remind the Syrians and Iranians of who is top military dog here, the polls show people do not accept Olmert's unilateral declaration of victory. They know what victory feels like – and it does not feel like this. Sixty-two per cent of people say that the Prime Minister did not lead the country well during the war and agree that Israel did not achieve any of its objectives.

The government, which refused, *as a matter of principle*, any negotiations or exchange of prisoners, will have to free a thousand Palestinians to recover Corporal Shalit from Hamas. Even more will have to be released to return the two soldiers Hezbollah kidnapped.

Olmert's standing in the polls falls steeply. The ratings of the Defence Minister, Amir Peretz, plummet even more dramatically. But this centrist government was elected only a few months ago, and does not have to face elections for a while.

The only option left for Olmert is try and win approval for his leadership both politically and diplomatically. To continue to cultivate the *fear* which is so much part of this country's psyche? Or, do the opposite and take some steps towards peace by talking to the Palestinians?

For the leader of Hezbollah, the outcome is the very opposite. Nasrallah is now the hero of all enemies of the Hebrew state. Iran is delighted with the performance of the militias it sponsors and subsidises. Teheran will continue to arm and train Hezbollah. This is the first Israeli-Iranian war, conducted through an intermediary.

Nasrallah himself is surprised by the way his small provocation led to war on such a scale. 'Our holy victory has been won because Allah willed it. It is a historical and strategic victory.'

And it was a real war.

The Israeli air force flew 15,500 missions over Lebanon.

Hezbollah fired 3,790 missiles.

42 Israeli civilians were killed.

1,070 Lebanese civilians were killed.

120 Israeli soldiers were killed.

Hezbollah claims to have lost only 65 men, but everyone knows that it is being economical with the truth. A more realistic figure is 500 dead on their side.

But Nasrallah now feels bold enough to predict a 'happy

ending' – well, a happy ending for him, the Iranians and their fellow-travellers: Israel will disappear.

'When their Vice-Premier Peres said it was "a struggle for life or death for Israel" he was right,' Nasrallah declares. 'He knows the resistance is gaining strength and that the Zionist entity has no future. If that country starts to lose faith in its military, it's the beginning of the end for the *entity*.'

Debate rages in the 'Zionist entity' itself. I see five different strands of opinion

The positives – there are not many of them:

'We inflicted heavy losses on Hezbollah, they lost 600 men and we destroyed their bunkers and much of their infrastructure,' says one military chief.

'We won the war,' says a political commentator for *Ha'aretz*.

The realistic optimists:

'We had to fight this war, we could not live with Hezbollah armed to the teeth on our border.'

'We were lucky that this war was against little Hezbollah and not against the Syrians. That gives us time to prepare and improve the army for the next war.'

The realistic pessimists:

'We should not have gone back into Lebanon after six years.'

'A mistake of historic proportions,' says another political commentator for *Ha'aretz*.

'For the first time we have a civilian government with a Ministry of Defence who can't read a military map between them.'

The very depressed – the great majority:

'The problem is not that we made mistakes but that we seemed to be unable to correct them as we went along. You can't always be saying 'sorry I made a mistake.'

'Our politicians are only thinking about their position and the position of their different parties.'

The fatalists:

'There will never be peace.'

'Because of its geographical position and the tensions that stem from that, Israel will never be able to exist as a normal country'

'It's hard to be rational when you are afraid.'

A black joke does the rounds on the internet.

We won! (Crossed out).

We drew. (Crossed out).

What matters is taking part.

A Day Later

It is now a time for funerals and peace.

In Jerusalem David Grossman says Kaddish, the prayer for the dead, in front of his son's coffin, which is shrouded in the flag of Israel. He refuses to speak of politics or to discuss the war, which ended a day after Uri and his three comrades were killed. He speaks only of his son.

'My family and I have already lost this war,' he says.

The writer, an embodiment of the conscience of Israel, will spend three months in mourning and in silence. Then he chooses the 11th anniversary of the murder of Yitzhak Rabin, a murder committed by a Jewish extremist who wanted to stop all negotiations with the Palestinians, to make an explosive speech, a furious tirade that would sound much like a war-cry were it not a desperate and bereaved man's appeal for peace.

Every November in Tel Aviv, a huge crowd gathers on what was the Square of the Kings of Israel, re-named Rabin Square. David Grossman is bitterly direct.

He accuses the leaders of Israel of playing on the fears and anxieties of the people. They are obsessed with the use of force *'but we have discovered in this war that military power cannot ultimately guarantee our existence'*. He accuses the politicians of betraying the ideals of the Jewish state – and they were good ideals. It was to be a just state, a democratic state that embodied Jewish and universal values. A light unto the Nations of the World.

'Rabin took the way of peace with the Palestinians not because he loved them or their leaders but because he understood that Israeli society could not survive in a state of permanent insoluble conflict,' David Grossman speaks from the very spot where Rabin made his last speech, moments before his assassin fired.

The writer has become a spokesman for the people.

'Speak to the Palestinians! Speak to them above the heads of Hamas! Speak to them, speak to them of their pain, of their wounds and recognize the suffering that they have had to endure too. The catastrophe that has come upon my family and myself in the death of our son Uri does not give me any special right to speak, but I think that the experience of his death, and of the loss it means to us, brings a desperate lucidity.'

Will anyone listen to him? On either side?

As Uri Grossman is buried, I walk through another cemetery, in Jerusalem. I am sad, as I too have suffered a loss, but not one out of time. Marcel Greilsammer, my uncle, will not celebrate his 104th birthday. He died yesterday, the day of the ceasefire. When I saw him for the last time, I thought that he was not much affected by the rockets falling all around him, but maybe this war was one too many, after living through a century of constant fighting.

Marcel chose a beautiful setting for his tomb. It is on top of a hill surrounded by cypress trees. From here, Jerusalem below looks magnificent and calm. The calm is an illusion.

It is like the Alsace Lorraine of our ancestors, I tell myself. Two peoples are fighting for the same small parcel of land.

Thanks and credits

Thanks to Dan Franck who gave me the idea for this book.

Thanks to the girls – Andrée Michèle Rubinstein, Béatrice Vallaeys and Delphine Lévy - for their reading and comments as ever.

Thanks to the boys at *Libération* for their support – Thomas Hofnung, François Sergent, Jean-Pierre Perrin and Didier François.

Finally special thanks to Jil – Paule-Henriette Levy, to my family and to my Israeli friends who tried to keep up my morale – Noemi Schory-Ben Nathan, Katri Schory, Shlomo Papirblat and Marius Shatter.

The publisher wishes to mention and thank

Copy editor Reuben Cohen.
Cover and graphics Sophie Clausen.
Typesetting Ray Buckland of Keyboard Services.

The map of the rockets and bombs on page 94 is copyrighted to Debka. We tried to contact them first for permission to use and secondly to give them a chance to respond to our critique. Any future editions will attempt to include their response.

Thanks to the Israeli Tourist Office for permission to use their maps.